my revision notes

Edexcel AS/A-level History

GERMANY AND WEST GERMANY

1918–89

Barbara Warnock

Series editors:
Robin Bunce
Peter Callaghan

HODDER EDUCATION
AN HACHETTE UK COMPANY

Acknowledgements
The Publishers would like to thank the following for permission to reproduce copyright material.

pp.69 & 75 From THE ORIGINS OF THE SECOND WORLD WAR by A.J.P. Taylor (Hamish Hamilton 1961, Penguin Books 1964, 1987, 1991) Copyright © A J P Taylor, 1961, 1963. Reproduced by permission of Penguin Books Ltd; **pp.73 & 76** From THE THIRD REICH IN POWER by Richard Evans (Penguin Books 2003). Copyright © Richard Evans 2005. Reproduced by permission of Penguin Books Ltd.

Every effort has been made to trace all copyright holders, but if any have been inadvertently overlooked, the Publishers will be pleased to make the necessary arrangements at the first opportunity.

Although every effort has been made to ensure that website addresses are correct at time of going to press, Hodder Education cannot be held responsible for the content of any website mentioned in this book. It is sometimes possible to find a relocated web page by typing in the address of the home page for a website in the URL window of your browser.

Hachette UK's policy is to use papers that are natural, renewable and recyclable products and made from wood grown in sustainable forests. The logging and manufacturing processes are expected to conform to the environmental regulations of the country of origin.

Orders: please contact Bookpoint Ltd, 130 Milton Park, Abingdon, Oxon OX14 4SE. Telephone: +44 (0)1235 827720. Fax: +44 (0)1235 400454. Email education@bookpoint.co.uk Lines are open from 9 a.m. to 5 p.m., Monday to Saturday, with a 24-hour message answering service. You can also order through our website: www.hoddereducation.co.uk

ISBN: 978 1 4718 7649 3

© Barbara Warnock 2017

First published in 2017 by
Hodder Education,
An Hachette UK Company
Carmelite House
50 Victoria Embankment
London EC4Y 0DZ
www.hoddereducation.co.uk

Impression number   10 9 8 7 6 5 4 3 2 1

Year   2021 2020 2019 2018 2017

All rights reserved. Apart from any use permitted under UK copyright law, no part of this publication may be reproduced or transmitted in any form or by any means, electronic or mechanical, including photocopying and recording, or held within any information storage and retrieval system, without permission in writing from the publisher or under licence from the Copyright Licensing Agency Limited. Further details of such licences (for reprographic reproduction) may be obtained from the Copyright Licensing Agency Limited, Saffron House, 6–10 Kirby Street, London EC1N 8TS.

Cover photo © Christian Mueringer / Alamy Stock Photo

Illustrations by Integra

Typeset in Bembo Std Regular by Integra Software Services Pvt. Ltd., Pondicherry, India

Printed in Spain

A catalogue record for this title is available from the British Library.

My Revision Planner

5 Introduction

1 The Weimar Republic, 1918–33

- 6 The creation of a republic, 1918–19
- 8 The Weimar Constitution
- 10 The features of the Weimar Republic's constitution
- 12 Opposition to the government: the legacy of war and defeat
- 14 Economic crises, 1918–23
- 16 Government responses to economic crisis
- 18 Opposition to the government: political extremism, 1918–23 (part 1)
- 20 Opposition to the government: political extremism, 1918–23 (part 2)
- 22 Controlling extremism, 1918–23
- 24 Policies for recovery, 1924–29 – the 'Golden Years'
- 26 Social and cultural attitudes and policies
- 28 The impact of and responses to the Great Depression, 1929–32
- 30 The collapse of democracy, 1930–33 (part 1)
- 32 The growth of Nazi support
- 34 The collapse of democracy, 1930–33 (part 2)
- 36 Exam focus

2 Nazi Germany, 1933–45

- 38 Establishing a dictatorship
- 40 The nature of Nazi government, 1933–39
- 42 Support for the Nazi regime
- 44 Opposition and dissent
- 46 Terror and repression
- 48 Nazi racial policies
- 50 Nazi policies towards women
- 52 Nazi education and cultural policies
- 54 Nazi economic policies, 1933–39
- 56 Government in wartime
- 58 The war economy
- 60 The domestic impact of the war
- 62 The 'Final Solution' and the Holocaust
- 64 Exam focus

3 Historical interpretations: How far was Hitler's foreign policy responsible for the Second World War?

- 66 The influence of German history on Nazi foreign policy
- 68 Hitler's role in shaping foreign policy
- 70 The contribution of other nations to the outbreak of the war
- 72 Why did Germany invade Poland in 1939?
- 74 Domestic reasons for the German invasion of Poland
- 76 Exam focus (A-level)
- 78 Exam focus (AS-level)

4 Democratic government in West Germany, 1945–89

- 80 Return to democratic government: the creation of the Federal Republic of Germany, 1945–49
- 82 The denazification policies of the Western Allies, 1945–49
- 84 Establishing democracy from 1949
- 86 Consolidation under Adenauer and Erhard, 1949–66
- 88 Economic recovery and the 'economic miracle', 1945–66
- 90 The nature of support for democracy in the FRG, 1949–66
- 92 Maintaining political stability under Brandt, Schmidt and Kohl, 1966–89
- 94 Surviving economic challenges, 1966–89
- 96 Political dissent and active challenge, 1949–89
- 98 The constitutional and legal response to political extremism, 1949–89
- 100 Changing living standards, 1945–89
- 102 The role and status of women in the FRG
- 104 The status of, and attitudes towards, ethnic minorities in the FRG
- 106 Exam focus

- 108 **Glossary**
- 111 **Key figures**
- 112 **Timeline**
- 114 **Mark schemes**
- 116 **Answers**
- 119 **Notes**

REVISED

Introduction

About Paper 1

Paper 1 Option: Germany and West Germany, 1918–89 requires a breadth of knowledge of a historical period, as well as a knowledge of the historical debate around the causes of the Second World War. Paper 1 tests you against two Assessment Objectives: AO1 and AO3.

AO1 tests your ability to:
- organise and communicate your own knowledge
- analyse and evaluate key features of the past
- make supported judgements
- deal with concepts of cause, consequence, change, continuity, similarity, difference and significance.

On Paper 1, AO1 tasks require you to write essays from your own knowledge.

AO3 tests your ability to:
- analyse and evaluate interpretations of the past
- explore interpretations of the past in the context of historical debate.

On Paper 1, the AO3 task requires you to write an essay which analyses the work of historians.

At A-level, Paper 1 is worth 30 per cent of your qualification.

At AS-level Paper 1 is worth 60 per cent of your qualification. Significantly, your AS grade does not count towards your overall A-level grade.

The exam

The Paper 1 AS exam and A-level exam each last for 2 hours and 15 minutes, and are divided into three sections.

Section A and Section B test the breadth of your historical knowledge of the four themes.
- Section A requires you to write one essay from a choice of two. Section A questions will usually test your knowledge of at least a decade. You should spend around 35 to 40 minutes on Section A – this includes making a brief plan.
- Section B requires you to write one essay from a choice of two. Section B essays usually tests your knowledge of a third of the period 1918–79, around 23 years. You should spend around 35 to 40 minutes on Section B – this includes making a brief plan.

Section C tests your knowledge of the debate around Hitler's foreign policy and the causes of the Second World War.
- Section C requires you to answer one compulsory question relating to two extracts from the work of historians. Questions will focus on the years 1979–97. You should spend around 35 to 40 minutes on Section C, and an additional 20 minutes to read the extracts and make a plan.

The AS questions are of a lower level in order to differentiate them from the A-level questions. You will find examples of AS and A-level questions throughout the book.

How to use this book

This book has been designed to help you to develop the knowledge and skills necessary to succeed in this exam.
- Each section is made up of a series of topics organised into double-page spreads.
- On the left-hand page, you will find a summary of the key content you need to learn.
- Words in bold in the main content are defined in the glossary.
- On the right-hand page, you will find exam-focused activities.

Together, these two strands of the book will take you through the knowledge and skills essential for examination success.

Examination activities

There are three levels of exam focused activities.
- Band 1 activities are designed to develop the foundational skills needed to pass the exam. These have a green heading and this symbol.
- Band 2 activities are designed to build on the skills developed in Band 1 activities and to help you achieve a C grade. These have an orange heading and this symbol.
- Band 3 activities are designed to enable you to access the highest grades. These have a purple heading and this symbol.

Each section ends with an exam-style question and model high level answer with commentary. This should give you guidance on what is required to achieve the top grades.

1 The Weimar Republic, 1918–33

The creation of a republic, 1918–19

REVISED

The collapse of the Second Reich

The monarchical political system of the German **Second Reich** began to change and then collapse in the final weeks of the First World War and the process of creating a republican system of government began. Germany shifted towards democracy and to some extent saw a social revolution with a weakening of aristocratic power. The German revolution was not a total revolution, however, and many elements of the old regime remained.

Key event	Date	Description	A democratic revolution	A social revolution?
The revolution from above	29 September to 3 October 1918	The generals advised the Kaiser to appoint a new civilian government and seek an armistice. On 3 October the government was created, led by Prince Max of Baden.	Authoritarian military rule was at an end. Reichstag deputies from liberal and socialist parties formed part of the new government.	The government was no longer solely aristocrats and *Junkers* but now contained workers too.
The revolution from below	31 October to 8 November 1918	A mutiny by sailors in Kiel rapidly spread to other German ports. The government began to lose control as soviets sprung up across the country, and there were riots in many major cities.	Many ordinary Germans were involved in the disturbances.	The sailors' and workers' soviets represented a new and radical form of political organisation.
The abdication of the Kaiser and the declaration of a republic	9 November 1918	**Paul von Hindenburg** advised the Kaiser to abdicate, and William II fled to Holland. **Friedrich Ebert**, leader of the SPD, became Chancellor of a government of SPD and USPD members.	The monarchy had come to an end, and the government was led by the largest party in the Reichstag.	The government was formed of representatives of the working class rather than aristocrats.
Armistice	11 November 1918	The new government signed an armistice agreement with the Allies.		
The revolution limited	10 November 1918 to January 1919	Ebert was anti-communist and determined to prevent the German revolution becoming a civil war. He thus did a deal with the army to gain their support (the Ebert–Groener pact) and called for early democratic elections.	Elections were held in January 1919 on the basis of universal suffrage. The elections produced a constituent assembly.	The social impact of the revolution was now limited: the *Junker* class remained dominant in the judiciary and the civil service and the army remained unreformed.

Spot the mistake

Below are a sample exam question and a paragraph written in answer to this question. Why does this paragraph not get into Level 4? Once you have identified the mistake, rewrite the paragraph so that it displays the qualities of Level 4. The mark scheme on page 113 will help you.

How accurate is it to say that Germany was politically unstable in the period 1918–33?

> Germany was politically unstable at the end of the First World War because one of the effects of the First World War on Germany was that there was a revolution. In Germany in October and November 1918 the generals stopped running the country. A new civilian government was formed. This was the revolution from above. There was also a rebellion among the navy starting in Kiel and mass desertions from the army. There were protests and strikes across the country and some soviets were established. The Kaiser also abdicated. This was the revolution from below.

Delete as applicable

Below are a sample exam question and a paragraph written in partial answer to this question. Read the paragraph and decide which of the possible options (in bold) is the most appropriate. Delete the least appropriate options and complete the paragraph by justifying your selection.

How accurate is it to say that defeat in the First World War was the main cause of political instability in Germany in the years 1918–33?

> The loss of the First World War was the main cause of political instability in Germany 1918 to a **great/fair/limited** extent. The impending loss caused political instability in 1918. Generals Ludendorff and Hindenburg realised at the end of September 1918 that Germany could not win the war and they relinquished power as they did not want to still be in charge when defeat came. The generals' actions triggered the political events that caused massive political instability and revolution in Germany. Impending defeat in the war was also one reason why sailors mutinied at Kiel, an act that kicked off the 'revolution from below' that saw the Kaiser abdicate and the Second Reich collapse. After the war had actually ended on 11 November 1918, the political instability continued as an unstable new government was blamed for the harsh terms of the armistice. It faced political threats from the right-wing extremists who accused it of having betrayed Germany. In 1918, therefore, defeat in the First World War was a **significant/moderate/limited** cause of political instability in Germany.

The Weimar Constitution

A new system

Following elections in January 1919, a National Assembly met in the city of Weimar to form an interim parliament and to agree a new constitution. The largest party in the Assembly was the SPD, which had won 38 per cent of the vote. SPD representatives wished to create a democracy which secured rights for workers but they had to co-operate with the other pro-democracy parties such as the Zentrum Party (Catholic Centre Party) and the DDP (German Democratic Party). A liberal democratic system with protections for workers was eventually agreed upon.

The Weimar Republic

This is the name often given to Germany between 1919 and 1933. It refers to a period of democracy in Germany and takes its name from the city where the new constitution was agreed upon. The Weimar Republic had two presidents: Friedrich Ebert (1919–25) and Paul von Hindenburg (1925–34).

The constitution

Some of the main features of Weimar's constitutional arrangements were as follows.
- A President was to be elected every seven years by universal suffrage, with the power to select and dismiss the Chancellor. The Chancellor formed the government.
- The President was Supreme Commander of the Armed Forces.
- The President had emergency powers under Article 48 (see page 10). The President could dissolve the lower house of the German parliament, the Reichstag, and call new Reichstag elections under Article 25 of the constitution. The new elections had to occur within 60 days of the dissolution.
- The Chancellor and government were accountable to the Reichstag and had to resign if they lost the confidence of the Reichstag.
- The Reichstag was to be elected every four years. There was universal suffrage for people over the age of 20.
- Elections were to be conducted using proportional representation: the minimum requirement for a seat in the Reichstag was just 60,000 votes across the entire country.
- The system was a federal one: Germany was divided into 18 regions or states, each of which had their own parliament and local powers. The state parliaments sent representatives to the Reichsrat, the upper house of the German parliament. The Reichsrat could propose amendments or delay legislation passed by the Reichstag.
- Referenda on single issues could be held if enough people petitioned for one.

The Bill of Rights

The Weimar Republic's constitution also included a Bill of Rights in which certain rights were guaranteed. These provisions included:
- freedoms of speech, association and religion
- the right to work – the government should ensure that everyone had a job or, failing that, provide financial assistance
- a provision which gave workers special protection in the new state
- welfare rights, e.g. protection for the disabled
- the right to property – this right was guaranteed and businesses could not be nationalised without compensation.

Mind map

Use the information on the opposite page to add detail to the mind map below.

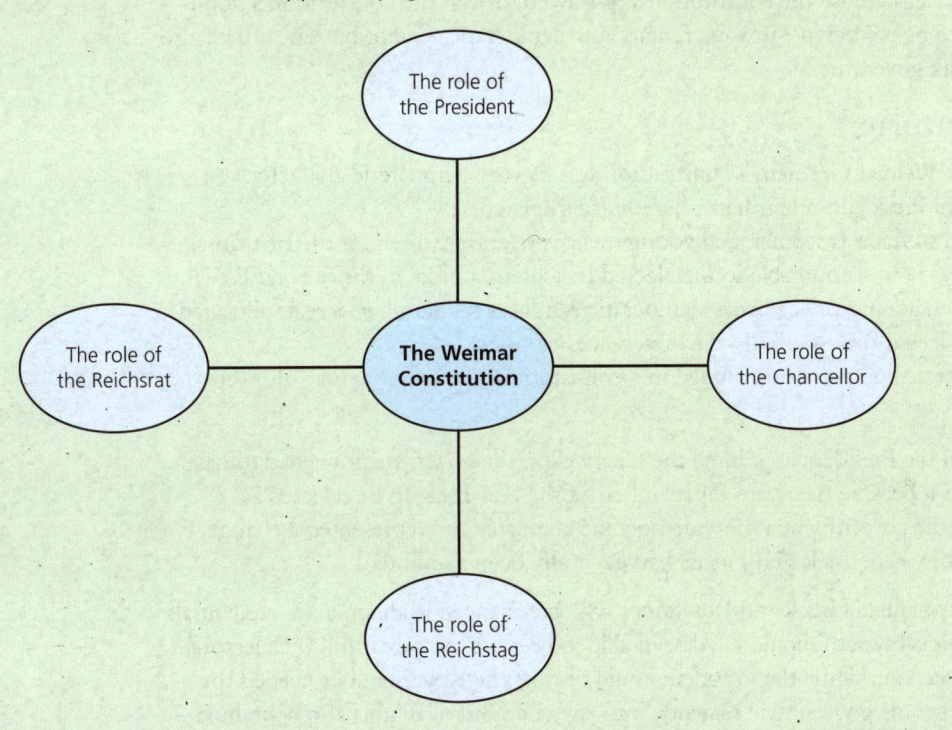

- The role of the President
- The role of the Reichsrat
- **The Weimar Constitution**
- The role of the Chancellor
- The role of the Reichstag

Recommended reading

Below is a list of suggested further reading on the topic of the establishment of the Weimar Republic.
- Chris Harman, *The Lost Revolution – Germany 1918 to 1923* (2008), pages 41–50
- Scott Stephenson, *The Final Battle: Soldiers of the Western Front and the German Revolution of 1918* (2009), pages 109–51
- Eberhard Kolb, translated by P. S. Falla and R. J. Park, *The Weimar Republic* (2005) pages 3–22

The features of the Weimar Republic's constitution

REVISED

The features of the Weimar Republic's constitution have been controversial. Did the system collapse after only 14 years because the constitution was flawed, or was the constitution a good one which was misused by politicians? It was a remarkably democratic system, but one which also tended to produce weak governments.

Democratic features

One notable feature of Weimar Germany's constitution was its very democratic character.
- There was an elected President rather than a hereditary monarch.
- There was universal suffrage as women and young men were enfranchised for the first time.
- The government was now accountable to the elected Reichstag, unlike in the Second Reich.
- Proportional representation produced very democratic results as the number of seats allocated in the Reichstag reflected almost exactly the preferences of voters.
- An element of direct democracy was included in a constitutional provision which allowed for referenda.

Furthermore, although the President appointed the Chancellor, the government needed to have Reichstag support, and it became the norm for members of the Reichstag to be selected as Chancellor. This gave the government a more democratic character and represented a change from the Second Reich, where unelected *Junkers* had generally been appointed.

The constitution also contained **checks and balances** which enhanced its democratic credentials. No one part of the political system should have been able to become too powerful: the electorate held the Reichstag to account, while the President could dismiss the Reichstag but needed the Reichstag's support to get the government's agenda into law. The Bill of Rights also contained liberal features that helped to support democracy, such as freedom of speech, which ensured a free press, and freedom of association, which meant that people were free to participate in politics via political parties, trade unions or pressure groups.

Emergency provisions

Under Article 48 of the constitution, the President had the power to rule via presidential decree in the event of an emergency. However, this power was checked, as the Reichstag could review and overturn any decree issued under Article 48.

Criticisms of the Weimar Republic's constitution

The Weimar Republic's constitution has been criticised for giving too much power to the President under Article 25 (which allowed him to dissolve the Reichstag) and Article 48, although both of these provisions contained limitations on the President's power. Proportional representation has been condemned by some for creating a fragmented party system which made it difficult to form durable coalition governments. It also meant that small extremist parties could gain representation and exposure: there were 20 separate coalition governments in Weimar Germany. Furthermore, some people in Germany objected to the socialist elements of the constitution, such as the right to work and the provision giving workers special protection.

Supporters and opponents of the Weimar Republic's constitution

Supporters	The pro-Weimar parties were the SPD, Zentrum Party and DDP; these parties won a majority in the 1919 elections.
	After 1920, the DVP (German People's Party) started to support Weimar.
Opponents	The conservative DVP initially opposed Weimar as they wished for a constitutional monarchy.
	The right-wing DNVP (German National People's Party) wavered in their support for Weimar and were mainly opposed prior to 1925 and after 1929.
	Many industrialists and business owners in Germany felt that the constitution gave too many rights to workers. By the early 1930s many of these people had stopped supporting the Weimar system as they felt it did not serve their interests.

Quick quizzes at www.hoddereducation.co.uk/myrevisionnotes

Complete the paragraph

Below are a sample exam question and a paragraph written in answer to this question. The paragraph contains a point and specific examples, but lacks a concluding analytical link back to the question. Complete the paragraph, adding this link in the space provided.

> How far do you agree that the Weimar constitution undermined stability in Germany 1919–29?

I agree to a limited extent that the Weimar constitution undermined stability in Germany in these years. With a proportional representation (PR) electoral system, the Weimar constitution meant that it was very difficult to form stable governments, as no party received enough votes to form a government on its own and unstable coalition governments were formed. These governments were short-lived. In addition, the PR system gave small political parties political representation in the Reichstag.

_____
_____

Eliminate irrelevance

Below are a sample exam question and a paragraph written in answer to this question. Read the paragraph and identify parts of the paragraph that are not directly relevant to the question. Draw a line through the information that is irrelevant and justify your deletions in the margin.

> How accurate is it to say that the Weimar constitution undermined stability in Germany in 1919–29?

It is not really accurate to say that the Weimar Republic's constitution undermined stability in Germany in 1919–29. Most of the problems that Weimar faced were nothing to do with the constitution. Although the constitution did add to political instability, as the PR system made it difficult to form durable governments, the main problems that Weimar faced were political extremism and economic problems that had nothing to do with the constitution. The political extremists included the Spartacists, named after a Thracian gladiator, and the Nazi Party, led by Hitler. Hitler was born in Braunau am Inn in Austria, and later lived in Vienna. His failed career as an artist had made him bitter. The existence of the extremists was more a result of defeat in the war and not really to do with the Weimar constitution. Use of PR for the electoral system made it easier for extremists to gain representation in the Reichstag, but PR is a very democratic election system that did not cause the existence of extremists. So use of PR did not mean that the Weimar Republic's constitution was flawed from the outset.

Opposition to the government: The legacy of war and defeat

Weimar Germany had been born of revolution, defeat and social and economic turmoil – and in its early years the Republic struggled to overcome various political and economic challenges.

The legacy of the First World War

Defeat in the First World War created a number of problems for the new democracy. Democratic politicians had no real option but to sign the armistice that ended the First World War in November 1918. The fact that they did so meant that many Germans unfairly blamed the democratic politicians for the defeat: some on the right labelled them the 'November Criminals'. The 'stab in the back myth', or *Dolchstoss*, which falsely portrayed the cause of the German loss to have been the revolution and betrayal by democratic and socialist politicians, was widely believed in some sections of German society and served to undermine support for Weimar Germany. When the Treaty of Versailles was signed, disillusionment with the new Republic set in because, despite the formation of the new democracy, a punitive peace treaty had been imposed. An additional negative legacy of the war was that its cost produced inflation, which contributed to post-war economic problems (see page 14).

The Treaty of Versailles

The Treaty of Versailles was the peace treaty between Germany and its opponents in the First World War.
- Germany's armed forces were restricted to 100,000 men in the army.
- Only six battleships were permitted, while no submarines or air force were allowed.
- Germany lost territory, including its overseas colonies and territory in Europe, such as West Posen and West Prussia to newly created Poland, and Alsace and Lorraine to France.
- The Rhineland, which bordered France, was **demilitarised** and the Saarland placed under **League of Nations** control.
- Union with Austria, *Anschluss*, was banned.
- Germany had to accept liability for the war in Clause 231, the 'War Guilt' clause, and pay compensation or reparations to the victors for damages incurred during the war.

The treaty was widely reviled in Germany as a *diktat*, or dictated peace.

Develop the detail

Below are a sample exam question and a paragraph written in answer to this question. The paragraph contains a limited amount of detail. Annotate the paragraph to add additional detail to the answer.

How accurate is it to say that opposition to the German state became progressively weaker in the period 1918–45?

> Opposition to the German state was strong at the start of the period. In the early years of Weimar, there was a lot of opposition to the state because the German public was shocked about losing the First World War and blamed the new government. In addition to this, many Germans were opposed to the state because they associated it with the hated Treaty of Versailles. For these reasons, opposition to the German state was strong at the start of the period.

Developing an argument

Below are a sample exam question, a list of key points that could be made to partially answer the question and a paragraph from the essay. Read the question, the partial plan and the sample paragraph. Rewrite the paragraph in order to develop an argument. Your paragraph should answer the question directly and set out the evidence that supports your argument. Crucially, it should develop an argument by setting out a general answer to the question and the reasons that support this.

How far do you agree that the most important factor driving opposition to the Weimar Republic 1919–32 was defeat in the First World War?

Key points
- The shock of defeat and ideas of the 'stab in the back' and 'November criminals'
- The Republic was born of defeat
- The Republic was born of revolution – political opposition
- The peace created opposition – the Treaty of Versailles

Sample paragraph

> Germany lost the First World War. This created opposition to the new democratic Weimar Republic as it was created in this time of defeat. People were shocked that Germany had lost, because the army had seemed to be in a strong position in the early summer of 1918. The shock meant that the public struggled to accept the defeat. Even though it was the old and not the new regime that had lost the war, the idea grew in right-wing circles that Germany had been 'stabbed in the back' – betrayed by democrats, communists, socialists and Jews who wanted to overthrow the government and the Kaiser. Pro-Weimar democratic politicians were thus blamed by some for losing the war. People associated the Republic with defeat and also the idea that politicians had sold Germany out by signing the armistice in November 1918.

Economic crises, 1918–23

REVISED

In 1923, many of the political and economic problems of Weimar Germany reached crisis point as inflation spiralled out of control, the German industrial region of the Ruhr was invaded and the Nazis attempted to overthrow the government.

The inflationary problem

Wartime and demobilisation inflation

- The First World War left Germany with high inflation. Much of the cost of the war had been financed by increasing the money supply and the German currency consequently declined in value.
- Wartime shortages exacerbated the problem and caused price rises.
- In the aftermath of the war, government expenditure remained high as the government had to support war widows, injured war veterans and millions of demobilised soldiers.
- Furthermore, the new constitution made social security a constitutional right, which obligated the government to provide support to the unemployed.

Reparations

- From 1921, the problem increased when reparations payments commenced.
- One difficulty Germany faced in meeting its reparations obligations was that most of the reparations had to be paid for in gold or foreign currency.
- As inflation increased and the value of the German currency weakened, buying gold or foreign currency to pay for reparations became an ever more expensive burden.
- In 1922, the German government sought to suspend their reparations payments, but were refused permission by the Allies.
- By early 1923, Germany was failing to meet all of its reparations obligations.

The Ruhr Crisis, 1923

In January 1923 the French and Belgian governments responded to German failure to meet all reparations payments by ordering the invasion of the Ruhr. Their armies occupied factories and mines and seized raw materials and goods in place of reparations. With government support, workers and business owners in the Ruhr followed a policy of passive resistance, refusing to co-operate with the occupying forces by going on strike. The German government paid the workers and compensated owners for lost revenue, thus adding to government expenditure. The situation in the Ruhr further damaged the German economy.

Hyperinflation

Inflation, which was already a profound problem following the war, ran out of control due to the Ruhr crisis as confidence in the German currency collapsed. Consequently, the mark became worthless. To try to meet spending obligations, the government printed more and more money, which added to the problem. In 1923, 300 paper mills and 150 printing presses worked 24 hours a day to print money. As the new government of Gustav Stresemann struggled to resolve the situation, the Nazis launched a failed Putsch in Munich in November 1923 (see page 20). In the end, the issue of hyperinflation was resolved (see page 16) – but not without causing a great shock to Germans, many of whom saw their savings eradicated or standard of living dramatically reduced. Debtors (who included many large business owners) benefitted, however, as the value of their debts was wiped out by hyperinflation.

Inflation in Germany 1919–23: marks needed to buy one US dollar

Apr 1919	Nov 1921	Aug 1922	Jan 1923	Sep 1923	Dec 1923
12	263	1,000	17,000	98,860,000	4,200,000,000,000

Establish criteria

Below is a sample exam question which requires you to make a judgement. The key term in the question has been underlined. Defining the meaning of the key term can help you to establish criteria that you can use to make a judgement.

Read the question, define the key term and then set out two or three criteria based on the key term which you can use to reach and justify a judgement.

> How accurate is it to say that the <u>main problem</u> facing the Weimar Republic between 1919 and 1923 was inflation?

Definition:
_____
_____

Criteria:
_____
_____
_____

Support your judgement

Below are a sample exam question and two basic judgements. Read the exam question and the two judgements. Support the judgement that you agree with most strongly by adding a reason that justifies the judgement.

> How accurate is it to say that the most significant problem facing the Weimar Republic in the years 1919–33 was inflation?

It is generally accurate to say that the most significant problem facing the Weimar Republic between 1919 and 1933 was inflation
_____
_____

While inflation was a difficulty, it was not the most significant problem facing the Weimar Republic between 1919 and 1933
_____
_____

Tip: whichever option you choose you will have to weigh up both sides of the argument. You could use phrases such as 'whereas' or words like 'although' in order to help the process of evaluation.

Government responses to economic crisis

The actions of Gustav Stresemann

As Chancellor, Stresemann helped to solve the crisis of 1923 by calling off passive resistance to French occupation in the Ruhr. This reduced the government's reparations payments and calmed the situation. Stresemann recognised that international confidence in Germany would only be restored if Germany met its obligations and so he restarted reparations payments. To pay for this, government spending was cut (700,000 state employees were sacked) and Stresemann worked to negotiate the Dawes Plan, which alleviated the burden of reparations payments and provided US loans and investment to assist the German economy.

In addition, Stresemann worked with banker Hjalmar Schacht and finance minister Hans Luther to resolve inflation. The old currency was abolished and a new currency, the *Rentenmark*, was established. One unit of the new currency was worth one trillion of the old. The new currency was guaranteed by linking it to German industrial and agricultural assets.

The Dawes Plan, 1924

Banker Charles Dawes led an international committee which redesigned reparations. The annual payment of gold marks was reduced to 1 million, rising to 2.5 million from 1929. An international loan was made available to help Germany pay.

Living standards during the early years of Weimar Germany

The hyperinflation crisis affected those with savings adversely, as their values were all but eradicated. The German middle classes often had substantial savings, and the decimation of these dramatically reduced their security and, in many cases, living standards. Those with debts, such as some businesses and many farmers, found their values substantially reduced, however, and in this sense their material position improved. High rates of inflation helped to ensure high levels of employment, which helped to maintain workers' living standards, as did new laws that protected their position. During the period of hyperinflation, wages did not keep up with prices, and so workers' standard of living did suffer in this sense. Generally, however, the position of workers improved in the early years of Weimar, and wages rose.

Support your judgement

Below are a sample exam question and two basic judgements. Read the exam question and the two judgements. Support the judgement that you agree with most strongly by adding a reason that justifies the judgement.

> How far do you agree that German government introduced effective economic policies in the years 1919–29?

To some extent the German government introduced effective economic policies in the years 1919–29
_____
_____

To a significant extent the German government introduced effective economic policies in the years 1919–29
_____
_____

To a limited extent the German government introduced effective economic policies in the years 1919–29
_____
_____

Tip: whichever option you choose you will have to weigh up both sides of the argument. You could use phrases such as 'whereas' or words like 'although' in order to help the process of evaluation.

Develop the detail

Below are a sample exam question and a paragraph written in answer to this question. The paragraph contains a limited amount of detail. Annotate the paragraph to add additional detail to the answer.

> How far do you agree that the actions of Gustav Stresemann were primarily responsible for creating stability in Germany by 1929?

As Chancellor and Foreign Secretary in the Weimar Republic, Gustav Stresemann took a number of actions which helped to create stability in Germany by 1928. Stresemann acted decisively in 1923 in ending the Ruhr crisis. This reduced government costs. He also took steps that helped to create economic stability by introducing a new currency, the Rentenmark, which helped to end hyperinflation and started a period of economic growth in Germany. In addition, Stresemann helped to create economic stability by negotiating the Dawes Plan.

Edexcel AS/A-level History Germany and West Germany 1918–89

Opposition to the government: political extremism, 1918–23 (part 1)

Political extremists from the right and left were opposed to democracy in Germany and constituted a major threat to it.

The threat from the extreme left

Some on the extreme left wished to see Germany become a communist state akin to the **Soviet Union** and sought the destruction of Weimar Germany.

The Spartacist Uprising, 1919

In January 1919, the communist political group the Spartacists took advantage of a large political protest in Berlin to launch an attempted communist revolution. President Ebert ordered the paramilitary *Freikorps*, volunteer groups of armed ex-servicemen, to crush the attempted rebellion. The leaders of the Spartacists, Rosa Luxembourg and Karl Liebknecht, were killed.

Strikes, risings and communist takeover

Widespread strike action and communist street violence contributed to the atmosphere of instability in Germany in the early 1920s. Communists also temporarily took control or rebelled in a number of areas of Germany: Bavaria in 1919, the Ruhr in 1920 and Saxony and Thuringia in 1923. With Ebert's support, the army and sometimes *Freikorps* acted to crush these rebellions.

Fear of communism

The activities of left-wing revolutionaries and the success of the communist takeover in Russia caused many to fear communist revolution in Germany. This fear of **communism** led some to overlook the threat posed by the extreme right – who, in reality, were the larger danger.

The threat from the extreme right

Many on the extreme right did not support democracy and tried to undermine or destroy the Weimar system.

The Kapp Putsch, 1920

Following an order to disband a *Freikorps* group as part of the disarmament process that occurred in Germany after the First World War, a group of right-wing politicians and soldiers seized control of government in Berlin for several days. The government fled to Stuttgart. The Putsch lacked support both from the general public and many in the elite, and collapsed. The Putsch is named after one of its leaders, Wolfgang Kapp.

White terror: assassinations and violence

Anti-Weimar paramilitary groups carried out a wave of political assassinations between 1919 and 1922 and created a destabilising atmosphere of violence on the streets of Germany as they launched violent attacks on political opponents. In total, 354 political assassinations were carried out by right-wing death squads, primarily the group Organisation Consul, including the murder of prominent politicians such as former finance minister and Zentrum Party member Matthias Erzberger in 1921, and foreign minister and industrialist Walther Rathenau in 1922.

Political assassinations

- Between January 1919 and 24 June 1922 there were a total of 376 political murders in Germany.
- 354 of these were committed by sympathisers of the right, with whom many judges sympathised. Of these murders, 326 went unpunished, and one life sentence and a total of 90 years in prison were handed out.
- 22 of these murders were committed by sympathisers of the left. Of these murders, four went unpunished, and 10 death sentences, three life sentences and a total of 250 years in prison were handed out.

Damaging ideas

The nationalist right did not just undermine Weimar through direct action: ideas such as the 'stab in the back' myth had a negative effect by making democracy appear weak and un-German and by portraying democratic politicians as traitors.

Lack of public support for democracy

Another problem faced by Weimar was that the new democratic system did not have wholehearted support of the majority of Germans between 1919 and 1923. The first election in 1919 produced a majority for the pro-Weimar parties, but the 1920 election saw their support slump to only 45 per cent.

Delete as applicable

Below are a sample exam question and a paragraph written in answer to this question. Read the paragraph and decide which of the possible options (in bold) is most appropriate. Delete the least appropriate options and complete the paragraph by justifying your selection.

> How far do you agree that the extreme right posed more of a threat to government in Germany than the extreme left in the years 1919–23?

In the early Weimar era, I agree to a **limited/fair/great** extent that the extreme right posed more of a threat to government in Germany than the extreme left. The extreme left was often perceived as more of a threat, and there were attempts to provoke revolution such as during the Spartacist Uprising in 1919. There was also a temporary communist takeover of power in Munich in 1919. Both the Spartacist Uprising and the Soviet Republic in Bavaria were defeated by the *Freikorps*. The extreme right also launched attempted seizures of power, such as during the Kapp Putsch in 1920 and the Munich Putsch in 1923. The Kapp Putsch was particularly serious, as those behind it succeeded in taking control of the central government for a number of days. The extreme right posed more a threat to democracy than the extreme left in the early years of Weimar because of the far higher level of political assassinations that they committed. In total, 354 political murders were carried out by the extreme right, including the murders of senior democratic politicians such as Erzberger and Rathenau. The extreme left carried out 22 political murders in the same period, which also undermined democracy, but not to the same extent. Furthermore, the extreme right promoted ideas, such as the 'stab in the back myth', that were a threat to democracy. The 'myth' involved the idea that Germany only lost the war because of the traitorous activities of democrats, socialists and Jews. Overall, in the early years of the Weimar Republic, I agree that the extreme right posed a greater threat to the democratic government than the extreme left to a **limited/moderate/significant** extent.

_____
_____

Establish criteria

Below is a sample exam question which requires you to make a judgement. The key term in the question has been underlined. Defining the meaning of the key term can help you establish criteria that you can use to make a judgement.

Read the question, define the key term and then set out two or three criteria based on a key term, which you can use to reach and justify a judgement.

> How accurate is it to say that political extremism posed <u>a significant threat</u> to the stability of the Weimar Republic 1919–29?

Definition:
_____
_____

Criteria:
_____
_____
_____

Opposition to the government: political extremism, 1918–23 (part 2)

The party that would later take over power and end the Weimar Republic, the National Socialist or Nazi Party, was founded in the context of the climate of political extremism that existed in Germany after the end of the First World War.

The origins of the Nazi party

The German Workers' Party (DAP) was founded by Anton Drexler in politically unstable Munich in the aftermath of the First World War. Despite the party's socialist-sounding name, Drexler's real agenda was nationalist, but he hoped to attract German workers away from support for socialism and communism and towards support for a nationalist agenda by addressing some of their material concerns.

Austrian-born **Adolf Hitler** was sent by the German army to report upon the DAP's activities. At this time the party was tiny and had very little impact but, interested in what he heard, Hitler joined the party and soon made an impact through his powerful oratory in speeches that condemned the Treaty of Versailles and blamed communists and Jews for Germany's problems. To emphasise its nationalist agenda, the party was now renamed the National Socialist German Workers' Party (or NSDAP, commonly referred to as the Nazis). In 1920, Drexler and Hitler drew up the party programme, the 25 Points, and in 1921 Hitler became leader, or Führer, of the Party.

Nazi ideology

The 25 Points contained the key elements of the Nazi party message. Hitler developed this ideology in speeches and his books *Mein Kampf* (1925) and *Zweites Buch* (1928).

- **German nationalism**: Germany should be strong, and all German-speaking peoples should be united in order to help maximise German strength. To develop German power, colonial expansion into Eastern Europe was needed. This 'living space' was called **Lebensraum**. In order for Germany to be strong, the Treaty of Versailles should be repudiated.
- **Racial ideas**: at the core of Hitler's ideas were false notions about race. These ideas had their origins in pseudo-scientific notions of the day. Hitler believed that differences between racial groups were profound and significant. Furthermore, he thought that races were organised into a hierarchy with Aryans, a Germanic-Nordic race, at the top. As a German nationalist, Hitler wanted Germany to maximise its strength, something he thought was only possible if a racially pure Aryan society was created in Germany. In his view, racial purity equalled national strength.
- **Anti-Semitism**: Hitler believed Jews to be a race and developed the notion that Aryan strength would be compromised and polluted through interbreeding with Jews, who he regarded as a vastly inferior racial group. Hitler also believed that Jews were engaged in a plot to sap Aryan racial strength through interbreeding.
- **Social Darwinism**: Hitler also subscribed to social Darwinist ideas. The notion of the 'survival of the fittest' was used as a moral principle by Hitler, who believed that not only did the fittest or strongest of species survive, but that it was morally right that the strongest triumph. Thus 'weaker' races and people should be eradicated.

Fascism

The philosophy of Hitler and the Nazis was fascist. Fascism combines an often racist nationalism with militarism and a belief in a strong state and strong authoritarian leadership. Fascism is anti-democratic and anti-socialist and also includes the idea of the need for some sort of national rebirth. One difference between Nazism and some kinds of fascism, such as Italian fascism, was the Nazis' obsession with anti-Semitism.

The Munich Putsch, November 1923

In the early 1920s, Hitler cultivated links with the elite in Munich and started to build up support for the party. He also worked with Ernst Röhm to develop an armed wing, the **Sturm Abteilung, SA**. In the atmosphere of crisis in Germany in late 1923 (see page 14), Hitler felt sufficiently confident to launch an attempted takeover of government. On 8 November in a beer hall in Munich, Hitler and Röhm, with the backing of ex-military leader General von Ludendorff, took control of a conservative political meeting and Hitler announced a national revolution. Hitler hoped to unite right-wing nationalists in an armed march to seize control of the country and provoke the army to rebel. In the event, some of the conservative politicians upon whose support Hitler had counted reported the plot to the authorities and the Bavarian police were able to stop the Putsch as its participants marched through Munich on 9 November. Hitler was arrested two days later and charged with high treason. He eventually received a five-year sentence, but served only nine months in jail.

Mind map

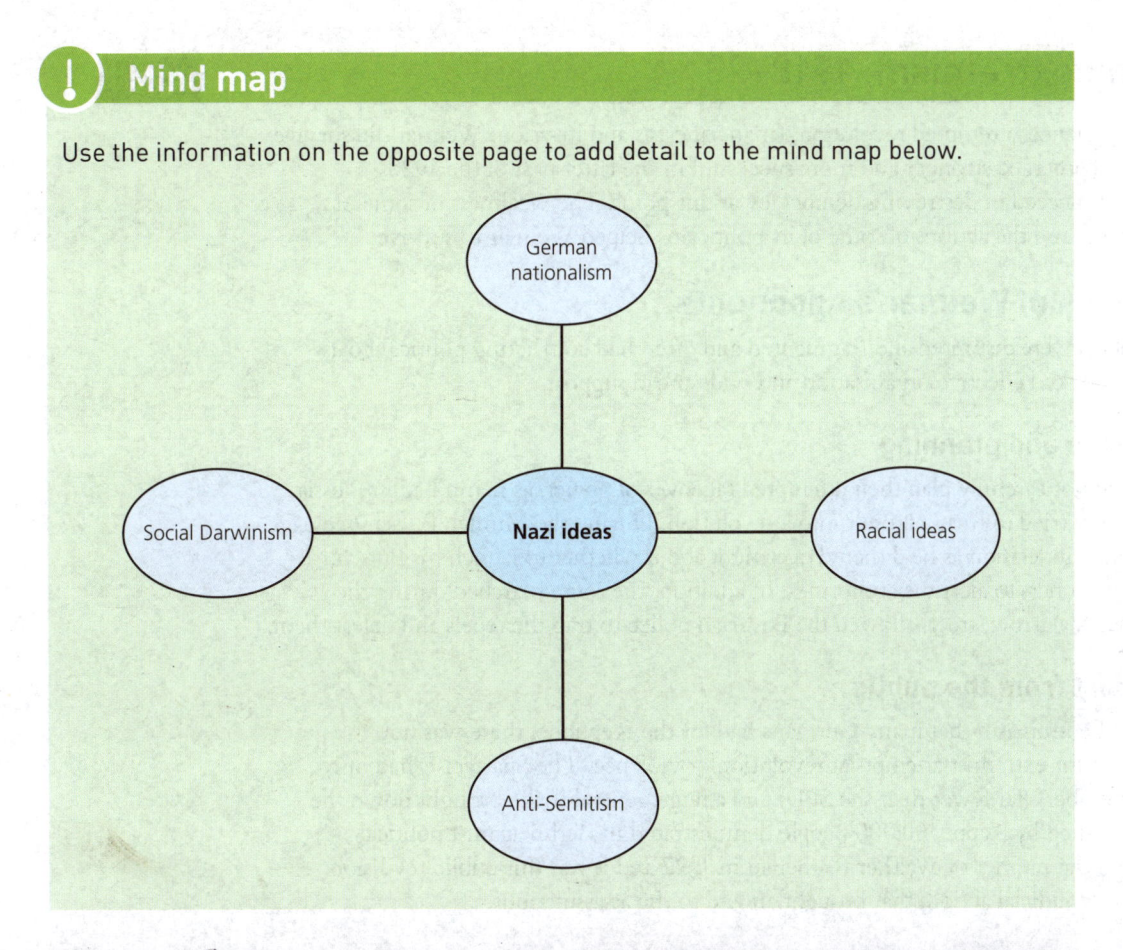

Use the information on the opposite page to add detail to the mind map below.

- German nationalism
- Social Darwinism
- Nazi ideas
- Racial ideas
- Anti-Semitism

Recommended reading

Below is a list of suggested further reading on this topic.
- Richard J. Evans, *The Coming of the Third Reich* (2004), pages 156–75
- Ian Kershaw, *Hitler 1889–1936: Hubris* (1998), pages 129–66

Controlling extremism, 1918–23

REVISED

Despite political violence, attempted revolution, financial crisis and invasion, Weimar did survive its early period and emerged stronger and more successful in the latter part of the 1920s. Extremists did not succeed in destroying democracy at this point. The weakness of some of Weimar's opponents and the actions of some of its politicians helped Weimar to survive.

The weakness of Weimar's opponents

Weimar's opponents were disunited and fragmented and often had conflicting political goals. Additionally, they lacked effective organisation and widespread support.

Poor leadership and planning

The Spartacists did not carefully plan their attempted takeover of power, as Lenin had in Russia, but opportunistically tried to turn a protest into a revolution. During the Munich Putsch (see page 20), Hitler exhibited indecision as he dithered overnight about whether to launch his Putsch, which gave time to others to alert the authorities. In addition, the route marched during the Putsch, down a fairly narrow street, allowed the Bavarian police to trap the rebels and defeat them.

Lack of support from the public

Despite the lack of enthusiasm that many Germans had for the Republic, there was not widespread support for extremist attempts at revolution or violence. The Spartacists had only around 15,000 members (far fewer than the SPD) and a huge general strike brought down the government established by Kapp. 700,000 people demonstrated in Berlin against political violence following the murder of Walther Rathenau in 1922 and it was this public revulsion, rather than police or judicial action, that brought an end to the assassinations.

The strengths of democracy

Democracy also had a series of strengths that helped it survive its difficult early years.

The actions of Ebert

President Ebert acted decisively and ruthlessly against the Spartacists in 1919 and other left-wing rebels such as those in the Ruhr in 1920. He also led the call for a general strike in Berlin during the Kapp Putsch. During the Munich Putsch, Ebert ruled under Article 48 briefly, which enabled him to take control of the situation.

Support of some of the elite

Despite the ambivalence of many in the elite for the new political system, at crucial points, certain members of the elite helped it to survive. The army enthusiastically crushed left-wing rebellions and the head of the army, General von Seeckt, did not endorse the Kapp Putsch, although neither did he oppose it. The army supported the government during the Munich Putsch. The civil service and banking community refused to cooperate with the Kapp government.

Support from the international community

The Dawes Plan of 1924 helped to stabilise the German economy and currency (see page 16). The international support that the plan received from politicians and bankers helped to restore confidence in the German economy for a time.

Support or challenge?

Below is a sample exam question which asks how far you agree with a specific statement. Below that is a series of general statements which are relevant to the question. Using your own knowledge and the information on the opposite page, decide whether these statements support or challenge the statement in the question and tick the appropriate box.

How accurate is it to say that it was the weaknesses of Weimar's opponents that allowed the Republic to survive until 1930?

	Support	Challenge
There were a number of attempts to overthrow the Weimar Republic, including the Munich Putsch, the Kapp Putsch and the Spartacist Uprising		
The international community supported Weimar's survival via the Dawes Plan and the Young Plan		
The actions of Ebert and Stresemann helped the Republic to survive		
The opponents of Weimar lacked public support before 1930		
There were a number of communist uprisings in the Weimar Republic		
The attempts to overthrow the Republic were badly organised		
Weimar's economy performed well between 1924 and 1929 and inflation was not a problem at this time		

Complete the paragraph

Below are a sample exam question and a paragraph written in answer to this question. The paragraph contains a point and specific examples, but lacks a concluding analytical link back to the question. Complete the paragraph, adding this link in the space provided.

How accurate is it to say that it was the weaknesses of Weimar's opponents that allowed the Republic to survive until 1930?

The weaknesses of Weimar's opponents in some ways contributed to the survival of the Weimar Republic until 1932. Weimar faced determined opposition from the extreme right and the extreme left. However, one weakness that the extremists faced was that before 1930 they lacked public support. This was shown by the general strike that occurred in opposition to the Kapp Putsch in 1920 and in the lack of public support for the Nazis during the Munich Putsch in 1923. In 1919, the communist group the Spartacists had tried to launch an uprising in Berlin but had not succeeded in gaining mass support. The moderate and pro-Weimar socialist SPD had far more support than the Spartacists. In addition, the murders carried out by extremists were generally opposed by the public, as a massive demonstration after the murder of Walther Rathenau in 1922 showed. Furthermore, Weimar's opponents were weak in the early years of the Republic because they were often badly organised and led. The Munich Putsch, for example, was not effectively planned and implemented by Hitler. Overall,

_____

_____

Policies for recovery, 1924–29 – the 'Golden Years'

REVISED

After the difficult early years of the new republic, subsequent years saw economic improvements and greater political stability. During this era, sometimes referred to as the 'Golden Years', support for democracy increased, the economy grew and Germany gained acceptance in the international community. However, underneath the apparently stable surface, Germany still had a great many problems.

Were the 'Golden Years' really so golden?

	Positive features	Negative features
Politics	**Increased political stability** • No Putsch attempts. • No political assassinations. • The creation of the **Grand Coalition** in 1928: this coalition, led by the SPD's Müller, was a coalition of the left, right and centre and commanded a secure majority (over 60 per cent) in the Reichstag. **Increased acceptance of democracy** • By the 1928 election 76 per cent of people supported pro-Weimar parties. • Support for the Nazis was very low: they obtained only 2.6 per cent of the vote in 1928. • A far-right coalition failed to get support in their anti-Young Plan referendum. **The role of Hindenburg** • Despite his authoritarian past, President Hindenburg, elected in 1925, supported the new constitution in the 1920s and in 1928 chose an SPD Chancellor, Müller.	**Immature party politics and unstable coalitions** • Political parties, who were unused to the real political power that the new constitution gave them, did not co-operate well or make the compromises that coalition politics required. The SPD were often reluctant to co-operate with others, while governments were sometimes brought down by trivial issues, such as the collapse of Luther's 1926 administration over the issue of what the German flag should look like. • Forming stable coalition governments proved difficult: the centre right and right wing could agree on domestic policies but not foreign policies, while the centre right and the left could agree on foreign policy but not domestic policies. There were consequently seven governments in the period 1923–29 and some governments did not have the majority support in the Reichstag. **Extremist support** • Support for extremists may have reduced but it remained worryingly high, with one-quarter of people voting for parties that wished to see Weimar democracy end: the KPD, German Communist Party, obtained 10.6 per cent of the vote in 1928. **The role of Hindenburg** • Hindenburg was obstructive to the idea of working with the SPD before 1928 and also had, until that time, insisted that the far right DNVP be included in coalitions.
Economics	**Economic growth and development** • By 1928, production equalled that of 1913. • By 1928, national income was 12 per cent higher than in 1913. • Certain sectors of the economy performed particularly well. Chemicals company IG Farben became the largest manufacturer in Europe. • Exports rose by 40 per cent between 1925 and 1929. • Loans from the international community and particularly the US financed the development of infrastructure in Germany: 25.5 billion marks were loaned 1924–30. • Inflation remained relatively low. • Unemployment ran at a relatively low rate for much of the 1920s. **Improved standards of living** • Wages rose every year between 1924 and 1930.	**A sluggish agricultural sector** • Agriculture was in recession from 1927. **Dependence on the United States** • It appeared to make sense to use US money to promote development and economic growth in Germany – but when the effects of the **Wall Street Crash** and the Great Depression started to affect Germany, credit dried up and the US sought repayment of loans. **Problematic unemployment** • Unemployment did not fall below 1.3 million and levels were climbing before the impact of US economic problems was felt. **Economic weaknesses** • The German economy suffered from underinvestment during this period. • The German economy did not perform as well as comparable economies, such as Britain and France. **Social tensions** • Tensions remained high between workers and business owners: industrial disputes were common and many industrialists resented the system of arbitration established to resolve disputes.

Quick quizzes at www.hoddereducation.co.uk/myrevisionnotes

Spot the mistake

Below are a sample exam question and a paragraph written in answer to this question. Why does this paragraph not get into Level 4? Once you have identified the mistake, rewrite the paragraph so that it displays the qualities of Level 4. The mark scheme on page 113 will help you.

How far do you agree that the German economy was in continual difficulties in the years 1919–32?

> I do not agree entirely with this. The economy of the Weimar Republic performed better in the years 1924–29 and before the Wall Street Crash it looked quite strong. Between 1924 and 1929 there was not a serious problem with inflation and while there was unemployment in Germany at this time, the level was not too high. The economy grew, and by 1928 its size had exceeded the size of the pre-war economy. The export sector increased by 40 per cent, showing that Germany had regained its role as a trading country. Certain areas of the economy, such as the chemical industry, performed very well. There was also investment in infrastructure. Because of the positive economic situation, living standards also rose in Germany between 1924 and 1929.

Support or challenge?

Below is a sample exam question which asks how far you agree with a specific statement. Below that is a series of general statements which are relevant to the question. Using your own knowledge and the information on the opposite page, decide whether these statements support or challenge the statement in the question and tick the appropriate box.

How far do you agree that politicians in Germany consistently pursued effective economic policies in the years 1923–45?

	Support	Challenge
Stresemann called off the passive resistance to French occupation in 1923, which helped restore some international confidence in Germany's economy		
Stresemann negotiated the Dawes Plan, which saw money for investment flow into Germany		
The international loans to Germany in the 1920s created a dangerous dependence on the United States		
Unemployment remained persistent throughout the 1920s		
The German economy did not grow as much as other economies between 1924 and 1929		
The German agricultural sector was in recession from 1927		

Social and cultural attitudes and policies

Weimar culture and society in the 1920s

Newly democratic Germany saw a flourishing of cultural experimentation and a more liberal and tolerant atmosphere. This has contributed to the creation of a positive perception of Weimar Germany. Society also reflected these values: gay culture burgeoned in Berlin, and some young women in cities were able to pursue careers and live in an independent manner. Many Germans did not regard these cultural changes positively, however, and came to associate the Weimar system with decadence and experimentation. Outside of large urban areas, most Germans still preferred traditional culture and traditional roles for women and did not tolerate homosexuality.

The position of women

In the years after the First World War, some young women were able to live a more independent and self-supporting way of life than had generally been possible before the war. More women attended university and worked in profession occupations. In big cities, and particularly in Berlin, young women dressed and behaved in a more relaxed way than previously (by, for example, smoking), and were to an extent more sexually liberated. Working-class women had often worked before the First Word War, however, so their position was not much altered. Furthermore, most German women continued to have traditional roles as wives and mothers within families, and many German women were hostile to the values of the young and single city-dwelling 'new women'.

The position of gay people

In Berlin in the Weimar era, gay culture was tolerated to a large extent, despite homosexuality being theoretically still illegal. Gay culture flourished in Berlin after the First World War, and there were countless gay bars and gay publications in existence in the 1920s and early 1930s.

Cultural experimentation

Weimar Germany led the world in cultural and artistic developments in the 1920s.

Weimar artistic culture

- In art, George Grosz and Otto Dix produced artworks that reflected on the impact of the First World War and satirised the *Junker* class and many features of Weimar society.
- In architecture and design, the hugely influential **Bauhaus** movement created modern designs for buildings, furniture and graphics.
- In music, American jazz became very popular and began to influence the sound of German popular music. There was a lively jazz scene in Berlin.
- In literature, Erik Maria Remarque's *All Quiet On the Western Front* (1929) examined the traumatic impact of the First World War on German soldiers.
- In cinema, Germany had a world-leading industry and **expressionist** works such as Fritz Lang's *Metropolis* (1927) were particularly influential.
- Satirical forms of cabaret were popular in Berlin.

Education in the Weimar Republic

According to the Weimar constitution, education in Weimar Germany had a moral purpose to encourage students' personal development and sense of civic responsibility, while also fostering a spirit of reconciliation with the peoples of other countries. It was also the goal of education policy to provide equal access to education to all students, regardless of their wealth. Free education was provided for all until age 14, but the goal of integrating schooling to ensure equal access (as outlined in the 1920 School Law) was never achieved at secondary level. At primary level, schools were not allowed to select according to ability or religious affiliation, but at secondary level some religious private schools remained. The most prestigious schools, grammar schools (*Gymnasia*), often remained fee-paying. A system of inspections was introduced, however, and moves to increase religious education were defeated. Some, such as Rudolph Steiner, experimented with very liberal educational methods.

The status of, and attitudes towards, ethnic minorities, 1918–32

Practising Jews in Germany formed about 1 per cent of the population. During the late nineteenth century, explicitly **anti-Semitic** and German nationalist political groups sprung up. Pseudo-scientific racial ideas that Europeans were racially superior to those peoples they colonised in, for example, Africa were also commonly held. The legacy of these attitudes was felt in the Weimar era. Jews had equal citizenship rights in Weimar Germany, but stereotypes and prejudice continued. Jews were informally excluded from certain professions, such as the judiciary, and there existed a perception of Jews as rich and greedy, despite the fact that 20 per cent of Jews in Germany lived in poverty. Racist attitudes about German 'superiority' continued in relation to the small number of black people, often jazz musicians, who lived in Germany at this time. The racial attitudes of most Germans were not that different from the attitudes of many Europeans at the time, however.

Quick quizzes at www.hoddereducation.co.uk/myrevisionnotes

Eliminate irrelevance

Below are a sample exam question and a paragraph written in answer to this question. Read the paragraph and identify parts of the paragraph that are not directly relevant to the question. Draw a line through the information that is irrelevant and justify your deletions in the margin.

> How far do you agree that the lives of women in Germany were transformed in the years 1918–33?

The lives of some women were transformed in the Weimar era in Germany. Some young women living in urban areas, particularly Berlin, were able to live an independent and single life in a way that had not been possible before the First World War. This was all part of the more liberal and tolerant culture in Germany, and particularly in Berlin. At this time there was a great deal of cultural experimentation in Germany, as can be seen in the artwork of Kirchener, the designs of the Bauhaus and in the development of cabaret as an art form. Furthermore, more women went to university and trained and worked in professions in this era. However, most women continued to occupy traditional roles within the family as wives and mothers, and many working-class women had worked before the Weimar era anyway, so the lives of these women were not transformed.

Recommended reading

Below is a list of suggested further reading on the culture of Berlin in the Weimar era.
- Christopher Isherwood, *Goodbye to Berlin* (1939)
- Peter Gay, *Weimar Culture – the Outsider as Insider* (1968), pages 102–18
- Eric D. Weitz, *Weimar Germany – Promise and Tragedy* (2007), pages 297–330

The impact of and responses to the Great Depression, 1929–32

REVISED

The economic impact of the Depression

Following the Wall Street stock market crash in the United States in October 1929, the American economy experienced a depression as bankruptcies and a banking crisis ensued. The German economy was heavily dependent upon US money and was therefore very exposed when US investment dried up and loans were recalled.

The German economy was severely affected:
- National income shrunk by 39 per cent between 1929 and 1932.
- Industrial production declined by more than 40 per cent.
- The number of unemployed rose to officially around 6 million by 1932 (the actual figure was probably higher). One-third of people of working age were affected.
- 50,000 businesses were bankrupted.
- In 1931, as the German economy collapsed, a banking crisis was triggered and five major banks went bankrupt. Other banks remained closed for three weeks.
- Homelessness and poverty increased and people's standard of living decreased – many felt insecure and desperate.

Responses to the Depression

Before 1931, the responses of the German government to the Depression served to deepen problems and increase political disillusionment. The members of Müller's Grand Coalition government disagreed over whether the response to the rising level of unemployment should be to cut welfare spending, and President Hindenburg refused to back his SPD Chancellor Müller over the issue – Müller did not support cuts.

Müller's government fell and was replaced by that of Heinrich Brüning of the Zentrum Party. **Brüning** lacked the support of the Reichstag and came to rely on President Hindenburg pushing through his measures using the emergency Article 48 provisions of the constitution. Brüning followed with policies of cuts and austerity in 1930, which deepened the Depression and increased poverty. He became known as the 'hunger Chancellor'. The Chancellor was more focused upon ending reparations payments (which he achieved in 1931 with the **Hoover Moratorium**) than upon dealing with unemployment, hunger and the shrinking economy. He did, however, begin a modest **public works scheme** after the banking collapse of 1931. This scheme was extended by Chancellor von Papen in 1932 and expanded further by Chancellor **von Schleicher** during his short-lived administration. Brüning's actions on the Depression could be characterised as 'too little, too late', and in failing to come up with effective solutions, the governments between 1930 and 1932 increased the crisis of democracy that contributed to Hitler's rise to power.

The effects of the Depression on living standards

The Depression had a catastrophic effect on living standards for workers, with around one in three people affected by unemployment. Reductions in the level of welfare support further increased the suffering and left many in desperate and even destitute circumstances. Shanty towns and soup kitchens sprung up. In the middle classes, some people were also affected by reduced wages and redundancies, and others lost their savings in the banking crash. Many business owners went bust.

Mind map

Use the information on the opposite page to add detail to the mind map below.

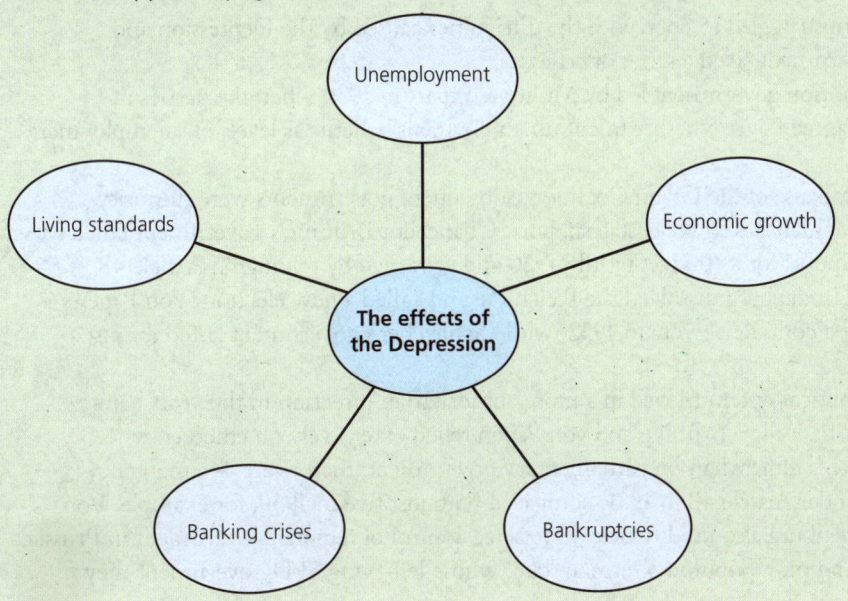

- The effects of the Depression
  - Unemployment
  - Economic growth
  - Bankruptcies
  - Banking crises
  - Living standards

Identify an argument

Below are a series of definitions, a sample exam question and two sample conclusions. One of the conclusions achieves a high mark because it contains an argument (an assertion justified with a reason). The other achieves a lower mark because it contains only description (a detailed account) and assertion (a statement of fact or an opinion which is not supported by a reason). Identify which is which. The mark scheme on page 113 will help you.

> How far do you agree that the economic policies followed by the Weimar governments 1919–33 were ineffective in dealing with the economic problems that Germany faced?

In conclusion, the governments of Weimar did not generally have effective economic policies. In 1923, inflation was ended through the introduction a new currency, the Rentenmark. Before this, inflation had run out of control and had reached the level of hyperinflation. People's savings were wiped out and the currency was worthless. The government's response to the Depression after 1929 was to do very little. Unemployment became very high, with one in three workers out of a job by 1932. The economy also shrank dramatically in size at this time.

The economic policies followed by the governments of Weimar were generally ineffective. However, they did have some successes, for example in ending inflation and introducing a new, stable currency in 1923. Furthermore, the inflationary policy followed before this was not completely ineffective, as it reduced the size of German debts and helped maintain employment. However, the policies followed during the Depression after 1929 were not generally effective. The government cut expenditure, which fuelled unemployment further. The ineffectiveness of the economic policies followed can be seen in the very high rate of unemployment by 1932, when one in three workers was without a job. In addition, the government did not manage to stop bankruptcies and the shrinking size of the German economy 1929–32. Measures that the government took, such as public works schemes, were too little, too late. Overall, the policies pursued by government in Weimar with respect to the economy were only partially effective, and in the face of the biggest challenge, the Depression, they were ineffective.

Edexcel AS/A-level History Germany and West Germany 1918–89

The collapse of democracy, 1930–33 (part 1)

The political impact of the Depression

The political system struggled to cope with the difficulties caused by the Depression and parliamentary government faced a series of crises.

- The Grand Coalition government led by Müller fell apart in 1930 when the parties in government disagreed over whether to cut unemployment benefits as levels of unemployment rose.
- Following the collapse of the Grand Coalition, subsequent governments were minority administrations which lacked Reichstag support. Chancellor Brüning's government failed to get Reichstag support for its budget in July 1930 and governed by relying on Article 48. Consequently, Hindenburg dissolved the Reichstag and called a new election. Von Papen's government lost a confidence vote in 1932, while Schleicher's government lasted for just a few months.
- The German political system moved in a more authoritarian direction in the years before Hitler became Chancellor. Brüning and von Papen relied extensively on emergency presidential decrees rather than on parliamentary government: there were 44 emergency decrees issued under Article 48 in 1931, compared with just five in 1930, for example. Von Papen and Hindenburg also used Article 48 to seize control of regional government in Prussia, still the largest and most populous German state, whose left-wing SPD government they wished to crush.
- Politicians did not take effective action to deal with the Depression. Brüning only started to act in June 1932 by launching modest reflationary schemes; his actions can be characterised as too little, too late. German people lost faith in their political system as politicians failed to help them effectively.
- Democratic norms began to break down as political violence returned to the streets of Germany. During the July 1932 election campaign there were 461 riots in Prussia, in which a number of people died. The SA were responsible for much of the violence as they participated in battles against communists. Street violence added to an air of instability in Germany, which served to increase people's discontent.

Weimar Chancellors 1928–33

- Hermann Müller: June 1932–March 1930
- Heinrich Brüning: March 1930–May 1932
- Franz von Papen: May 1932–November 1932
- Kurt von Schleicher: December 1932–January 1933

Spectrum of importance

Below are a sample exam question and a list of general points which could be used to answer the question. Use your own knowledge and the information on the opposite page to reach a judgement about the importance of these general points to the question posed. Write numbers on the spectrum below to indicate their relative importance. Having done this, write a brief justification for your placement, explaining why some of these factors are more important than others. The resulting diagram could form the basis of an essay plan.

How far were economic factors the main reason for the weakness of Weimar democracy in the years 1929–32?

1. Economic factors
2. Lack of public support for democracy
3. The actions of the conservative elite
4. The role of war and defeat

Least important ←──────────────────────────────────────→ Most important

Turning assertion into argument

Below are a sample exam question and a series of assertions. Read the exam question and then add a justification to each of the assertions to turn it into an argument.

How far were economic factors the main reason for the weakness of Weimar democracy by 1932?

The effects of the Depression in Germany had undermined democracy there by 1932 because

_____

_____

In addition, the actions of some members of the conservative elite undermined democracy in Germany by

_____

_____

Furthermore, the situation in which the Weimar Republic had been founded arguably undermined democracy from the start in the sense that

_____

_____

Edexcel AS/A-level History Germany and West Germany 1918–89 31

The growth of Nazi support

In 1928, the Nazis were a fringe party with minimal support and yet only four years later they had become the most popular political party in Germany, winning more than 37 per cent of the vote in the July 1932 election. The economic and political crisis that Germany experienced made the Nazis and their message much more appealing.

The Depression and subsequent political crisis provided an opportunity for the Nazis. It was easy for them to attack the Weimar government and more people were now open to hearing the Nazis' message. As the Depression hit, the party's electoral success dramatically increased, as did the size of their membership, which was around 2 million by early 1933. The SA grew from 70,000 members in 1931 to 170,000 in 1932. Members were attracted to Nazi party organisations such as its young wing, the Hitler *Jugend* (Hitler Youth). Uniforms, activities and hiking appealed to young members while the frequently unemployed members of the SA were given a sense of purpose and an outlet for some of their frustrations in the violent ethos of the organisation.

Nazi party vote, Reichstag elections

Election date	1928	1930	July 1932*
Percentage of the vote	2.6%	18.3%	37.3%
Number of seats	12	107	230

*After these elections, the Nazi party was the largest in the Reichstag.

It was the Nazis' popularity in elections and their creation of a mass-membership organisation that put Hitler in contention for the Chancellorship of Germany.

The demographics of Nazi voters and Nazi members

- A much larger number of people voted for the Nazi party than were members.
- Nazi members were most likely to be young (two-thirds of members in 1930 were aged under 40) and male, partly because the party did not encourage active female participation.
- Women were more likely to vote for the party than men, however. Hitler had some success in appealing to women who had not previously voted – traditionally minded conservative women who had never liked democracy or Weimar.
- Catholics were less likely to support the party than Protestants as the majority of Catholic voters always supported the Zentrum Party.
- Urban dwellers were less likely to vote for the Nazis.
- Working-class people formed the largest number of Nazi party members at 31 per cent of members, but were on average less likely to be a member of the party than most other social classes. This apparent paradox can be accounted for, as the working class formed by far the largest social group in Germany: 46 per cent of the population were working class.
- In contrast, office workers and the self-employed were over-represented as party members.

The impact of propaganda

Nazi propaganda was tailored to different audiences to try to maximise their support. So, for example:

- messages about bread and work were deployed in working-class areas
- messages about Weimar's supposedly lax moral standards were tailored to conservative mothers
- anti-Semitism was often emphasised in rural areas.

The Nazis used posters, leaflets, rallies and speeches to get their message across, as well as modern technology such as radio and film. Rallies were designed to provoke an emotional response in participants through their orchestration of image, sound and emotive messages. The Nazis also benefitted from their association with the DNVP as their leader, Alfred Hugenberg, put his media empire of various newspapers and radio stations at the service of Nazi propagandists. The impact of propaganda was important, but it should be noted that the Nazis' vote increased dramatically even in areas which they didn't target with propaganda.

Hitler's appeal

The Nazi head of propaganda, Joseph Goebbels, cultivated an image for Hitler as Germany's heroic saviour. The image of Hitler as a strong, decisive leader in a time when politicians seemed weak and ineffective was very appealing. This 'Hitler myth' helped to gain support for Hitler and the Nazis. Hitler ran against Hindenburg in the presidential election of 1932 and his campaign 'Hitler over Germany' portrayed him as dynamic and modern, harnessing modern technology, such as radio, to put his message across, and travelling via aeroplane from region to region to campaign. Despite his eventual loss to Hindenburg, Hitler came second in the election and had established himself as a credible political leader.

Establish criteria

Below is a sample exam question which requires you to make a judgement. The key term in the question has been underlined. Defining the meaning of the key term can help you establish criteria that you can use to make a judgement.

Read the question, define the key term and then set out two or three criteria based on a key term, which you can use to reach and justify a judgement.

> How accurate is it to say that the <u>main reason</u> for the level of support for the Nazi Party in Germany 1922–32 was the appeal of Hitler?

Definition:
_____
_____

Criteria:
_____
_____
_____

Reach a judgement

Having defined the key term and established a series of criteria, you should now make a judgement. Consider how far the level of support the Nazis in Germany achieved was because of the appeal of Hitler, according to the criteria. Summarise your judgements below.

Criteria 1:
_____
_____

Criteria 2:
_____
_____

Criteria 3:
_____
_____

The collapse of democracy, 1930–33 (part 2)

Hitler's appointment to power

Hitler and the Nazis were able to capitalise upon the Depression and political crisis to gain the support that put Hitler in contention for the Chancellorship of Germany. President Hindenburg resisted appointing Hitler after the July 1932 election, however, despite the Nazis electoral success. Hitler was offered the vice-Chancellorship, but refused the offer – he held out to become Chancellor. Mass popularity was not sufficient for Hitler to be appointed and, crucially, it was the support that he received from some members of the political and economic elite that eventually led to his appointment.

- Pressure was applied on President Hindenburg by a number of influential industrialists and bankers who in 1932 urged him to appoint Hitler Chancellor. These included Hjalmar Schacht, the architect of the scheme to restore the German currency in 1923, and industrialists I. G. Farben and Krupp.
- Von Papen schemed against Chancellor von Schleicher, who was appointed in November 1932. Von Papen and others around him, such as Hindenburg's son Oscar and his state secretary, Otto Meissner, worked to persuade Hindenburg to appoint Hitler as Chancellor. Von Papen's plan involved his own appointment as Vice-Chancellor – Nazi members of the Cabinet were to be a minority. Von Papen wanted to use Hitler's popular support to give the legitimacy that his own government had lacked in 1932. Von Papen assumed that he would be able to control Hitler and after Hitler's appointment he crowed, 'We've hired him'.
- Many members of the conservative political and economic elite, including Hugenberg and steel manufacturer Thyssen, contributed to the Nazi party's funds.
- As the state of economic and political crisis continued, many conservatives feared a communist takeover – the KPD had seen its vote share increase from 3.2 million in 1928 to 5.9 million in November 1933. It was the Nazis' determination to smash the communists that caused some conservatives to back Hitler.
- Hindenburg eventually appointed Hitler to government in January. This followed von Schleicher's failed plan to attain an element of popular legitimacy for his government by splitting the Nazi movement and trying to work with trade unions. Von Papen's government had completely failed to gain Reichstag support, and von Schleicher had no more success.
- Hindenburg at this point finally relented and appointed Hitler. Despite a decline in the Nazis' vote share in the November 1932 election (from 37 per cent to 32 per cent), the party was still the largest in the Reichstag.

German conservatives

German conservatives were from the old *Junker* elite or the new business class. Like the Nazis, they had nationalist leanings, a desire for more authoritarian government and a hatred for socialists and communists.

Factors in Hitler's appointment to power

On 30 January 1933, Hitler was appointed as Chancellor of Germany, with von Papen as Vice-Chancellor, in a cabinet that only contained two other Nazi members.

The economic depression and the failure of politicians to deal effectively with it gave Hitler an opportunity and caused more people to listen to his message. Many were profoundly disillusioned with Weimar democracy, which was not strongly entrenched and which never appeared to have worked very effectively. The Nazis saw their support rise dramatically until they were the most popular political party. Supported by some conservatives who saw the Nazis as a way of creating a populist authoritarian government, Hindenburg was eventually persuaded to appoint Hitler as Chancellor.

Other factors contributing to Hitler's appointment to power included:
- Hitler's personal role (as a charismatic leader and tactician)
- Nazi propaganda
- SA violence.

Identify the concept

Below are four sample exam questions based on some of the following concepts:
- **Cause** – questions concern the reasons for something, or why something happened
- **Consequence** – questions concern the impact of an event, an action or a policy
- **Change/continuity** – questions ask you to investigate the extent to which things changed or stayed the same
- **Similarity/difference** – questions ask you to investigate the extent to which two events, actions or policies were similar
- **Significance** – questions concern the importance of an event, an action or a policy.

Read each of the questions and work out which of the concepts they are based on.

How far do you agree that Weimar democracy was always likely to fail?

How accurate is it to say that the rise in unemployment was the most important consequence of the economic problems that Germany faced 1922–32?

How accurate is it to say that the lack of support for democracy from Weimar's elite was responsible for Hitler's appointment to power?

How far did the level of support for democracy in Germany change in the years 1919–32?

Developing an argument

Below is a sample exam question, a list of key points that could be made to partially answer the question, and a paragraph from the essay. Read the question, the partial plan and the sample paragraph. Rewrite the paragraph in order to develop an argument. Your paragraph should answer the question directly and set out the evidence that supports your argument. Crucially, it should develop an argument by setting out a general answer to the question and the reasons that support it.

How far did the level of support for democracy in Germany change in the years 1919–32?

Key points:
- Lack of support for democracy in the years of Weimar – post First World War
- Increase in support for democracy as the political and economic situation improved mid-1920s
- Decline in support for democracy after 1929 – economic, social and political effects of the Depression

Sample paragraph

> The level of support varied. From 1924, the economic and political situation began to stabilise. The new currency was stable, and inflation had been brought under control. The Dawes Plan of 1924 saw American money invested in Germany, and the economy and prosperity grew. Unemployment, while never that low, was not a major problem. In politics, there were no further attempted putsches after the November 1923 Munich Putsch and no further major political assassinations. Politicians, such as Stresemann, who had been opposed to Weimar democracy in the early years of the Republic, now were working hard to support it. All of this caused support to grow.

Exam focus

REVISED

Below is a Level 5 answer to an A-level question. Read it and the comments around it.

> How accurate is it to say that by 1929, Germany was economically strong and politically stable?

To some extent Germany was economically strong and politically stable by 1929, although the outward signs of strength and stability masked serious underlying problems. By 1929, the country appeared to have recovered economically from the First World War, and the political situation seemed more stable than in the early years of the Republic. However, economic dependence on America and the fragility of Weimar democracy were serious weaknesses.

This introduction directly addresses the question.

In some respects, Germany was politically stable by 1929, particularly in comparison with the early years of the Weimar Republic. Political violence had dramatically reduced and political assassinations no longer occurred. The murder of key democratic politicians, such as Erzberger and Rathenau, in the early years of the Republic had created an atmosphere of instability and fear. By 1929, however, public opposition to the extremists who were responsible for the assassinations had caused them to cease, which increased the strength and stability of Germany at this time. In addition, the attempted Putsches and revolutions that had occurred in Germany between 1919 and 1923, such as the Kapp Putsch of 1920, had also now stopped. The political system seemed stronger and more stable as, by 1929, there were no longer violent attempts to overthrow it. The Weimar political system was also more widely accepted at this time by the public than had been the case before 1924. A sizeable majority of people now supported pro-democracy parties, unlike in the first years of Weimar, and in the 1928 election, the anti-democratic fascist Nazi Party only received 2.8 per cent of the vote. Politics in Germany also seemed more stable by 1929 in that political parties from the left and the right were able to come together and form a strong coalition government in Müller's 'Grand Coalition' in 1928. This socialist-led government included some right-wing parties and politicians, and unlike many of the previous governments of Weimar it was able to command a secure majority in the Reichstag. Before 1928, governments in Weimar had often been unstable and short-lived coalitions, and politicians struggled to co-operate with each other. The accession to power of the Grand Coalition seemed to show that German politics was now in a period of stability.

Accurate detail is used.

In economic terms, Germany appeared to be fairly strong by 1929. The hyperinflation crisis of 1923 was long over, and inflation had not returned as a significant problem. The economy was growing and its size had recovered to pre-war levels. Furthermore, unemployment was relatively low, and certainly not at the problematic levels that it was later to reach. By 1929, the German economy had received a large amount of investment and loans, particularly from the United States, and new sectors of the economy, such as chemicals, experienced strong growth. Wages in Germany also grew during the 1920s so that by 1929, most people's standards of living had improved compared to the immediately post-war period. Thus in economics, by 1929, Germany appeared fairly strong and stable, with a growing economy and a high level of investment.

Despite all of these positive developments, by 1929 Germany was not as strong and stable as it appeared. Even if the level of public support for the Weimar system had increased, there were still many people who supported anti-Weimar parties. The Communists, for example, received about 10 per cent of the vote. In 1929, the increase in support for Weimar was a fairly recent development, which was a source of possible instability. The persistence of a minority hostile to Weimar also suggested this. Another political issue that reduced the

The other side of the argument is explained and considered.

Quick quizzes at www.hoddereducation.co.uk/myrevisionnotes

strength and stability of Germany was that support for Weimar's democratic system among many powerful people was not very strong. Judges, for example, had shown this in the lenient sentences that were handed down to those who tried to overthrow the system during the Kapp and Munich Putsches. Many in the army and the upper classes were also not strong supporters of democracy. By 1929 some industrialists were becoming increasingly hostile to the Weimar system, feeling that it had benefitted workers too much. All of this created instability within Germany.

In some ways, Germany's economy was not strong and stable at all, in spite of positive developments up to 1929. Unemployment may not have been as high as it later became but it remained persistent, and economic growth was not that strong compared with other similar countries, such as Britain and France. In some areas, such as agriculture, depression had started in 1927, causing political frustration and hardship in rural areas. In the 1928 elections the Nazi Party managed to pick up a considerable number of votes in those areas affected, although they did not do well overall. A major potential source of weakness and instability by 1929 were the huge levels of loans that had flowed into Germany from the United States due to the Dawes Plan of 1924. This money had allowed greater investment in industry and made it easier for Germany to meet its reparations payments. However, it created a great and unstable dependence on the United States, which ultimately proved disastrous for the German economy after the effects of the Depression started to hit in late 1929.

Overall, there were many positive developments in Germany by 1929 which did indicate that, at least compared to the early years of the Weimar Republic, Germany was fairly strong and stable. Politics was more peaceful and effective and the Weimar system was more widely supported. The economy was growing and the inflation problem had been solved. However, significant numbers of people were still opposed to Weimar's system, and some powerful people, including high-ranking members of the army, were not supporters of democracy. The economy also had a dangerous dependence on US money. Germany was not therefore, entirely strong and stable by 1929.

This essay scores highly as it is very focused upon the question and establishes criteria to assess the issue of whether Germany was strong and stable by 1929. The essay also contains accurate detail and a clear and well-sustained argument in answer to the question.

Reverse engineering

The best essays are based on careful plans. Read the essay and the comments and try to work out the general points of the plan used to write the essay. Once you have done this, note down the specific examples used to support each general point.

AS-level questions

Were political divisions the main reason for the failure of the Weimar Republic in the years 1919–33?

Was outrage over the Treaty of Versailles the main reason for opposition to the Weimar Republic in the years 1919–32?

How far do you agree that economic problems were responsible for political instability in the Weimar Republic in the years 1918–32?

2 Nazi Germany, 1933–45

Establishing a dictatorship

REVISED

When Hitler was appointed Chancellor in January 1933, he was not dictator of Germany. By March 1933, Hitler had removed many of his political opponents, ended democracy and was dictator. Some have argued the state was now totalitarian. A number of events helped Hitler:

The Reichstag Fire, 27 February 1933

A communist, Marinus van der Lubbe, is thought to have set fire to the Reichstag building. Hitler and the Nazis stated that the fire was a communist conspiracy, when in fact the evidence points to van der Lubbe acting alone.

The Reichstag Fire Decree, 28 March 1933

Following the fire, President Hindenburg issued a decree (the Law for the Protection of People and State, or Reichstag Fire Decree), which suspended the civil rights parts of the Weimar constitution. The police and secret police now had the right to arrest people for any reason or none, and people could be held in captivity indefinitely. Mass arrests of communists, socialists and trade unionists followed.

Elections, 5 March 1933

The Reichstag elections of March 1933 were conducted in an atmosphere of violence and intimidation. The result was an increased vote share for the Nazis (43.5 per cent) and a Reichstag majority for the Nazi Party and their supporters. The SA harassed and attacked the KPD and SPD and many members of the KPD had been arrested before the election.

The opening of Dachau, 20 March 1933

Dachau, near Munich, was the first **concentration camp**. The Nazis' political opponents were imprisoned there.

Potsdam Day, 21 March 1933

A 'day of national unity' was held at **Potsdam**. Hindenburg and Hitler appeared before huge crowds together, to send out a message of Nazi and conservative unity.

The Enabling Act, 24 March 1933

Hitler now moved to take dictatorial powers, and asked the Reichstag to pass a law which would give him the power to rule by decree. The Enabling Act was passed by 444 votes to 94, with only the SPD opposing it. Members of the KPD were banned.

Factors enabling Nazi consolidation of power

Terror

- 100,000 political opponents of the Nazi party were imprisoned between 1933 and 1934.
- Concentration camps were opened and, in Berlin, hundreds of socialists who resisted arrest were murdered.
- The KPD were banned shortly after the Reichstag Fire, trade unions were all closed down on 1 May 1933, the SPD was banned in June 1933 and all other political parties were banned from July 1933.
- Hundreds of left-wing newspapers were closed.

In July 1934, Hitler ordered the murder of a number of political opponents and even supporters who he believed to be a threat, such as Ernst Röhm of the SA, on the **Night of the Long Knives**.

The support of the conservative elite

The Nazis consolidated their power thanks to the support of their conservative allies in the Reichstag. Further support from the conservative elite came from many industrialists who bankrolled the Nazis during the March 1933 election.

Propaganda

Goebbels's propaganda portrayed the government's actions as necessary to deal with a national emergency. Potsdam Day was an orchestrated piece of propaganda aimed at demonstrating the unity and popularity of the government.

An illusion of moderation

The Reichstag Fire Decree and Enabling Act gave created a (false) impression of the legality of the Nazis' actions. In addition, the **Concordat** with the Catholic Church of 20 July 1933 was designed to reassure Catholics.

Gleichschaltung

The Nazis also consolidated power through a process of **Gleichschaltung**, or co-ordination. A law of 7 April 1933 removed Jews and political opponents of the Nazis from the civil service, schools and courts. A Nazi labour organisation, the *Deutsche Arbeitsfront* (DAF) was established. The Nazis also moved to seize control of local government.

Spectrum of importance

Below are a sample exam question and a list of general points which could be used to answer the question. Use your own knowledge and the information on the opposite page to reach a judgement about the importance of these general points to the question posed. Write numbers on the spectrum below to indicate their relative importance.

Having done this, write a brief justification of your placement, explaining why some of these factors are more important than others. The resulting diagram could form the basis of an essay plan.

How significant was the use of terror in the years 1933–34 in establishing the power of the Nazi regime?

1. Impact of the Reichstag Fire
2. The Enabling Act
3. Imprisonment and execution of opponents
4. Propaganda
5. Support given by conservatives and Catholics

Least important ←———————————————————→ Most important

Develop the detail

Below are a sample exam question and a paragraph written in answer to this question. The paragraph contains a limited amount of detail. Annotate the paragraph to add additional detail to the answer.

How far do you agree that the Nazi regime in 1933 was a totalitarian state?

> In many respects the Nazi regime in 1933 could be described as a totalitarian state. In the early period of Nazi rule, the Nazis eliminated much of the opposition to their rule and created a dictatorship which had totalitarian features. The opposition were persecuted and many freedoms were removed. People were not able to protest or oppose. The Nazis created a one-party state and Hitler was given dictatorial powers after the Reichstag Fire. In these ways, the basis for a totalitarian state was established in 1933.

The nature of Nazi government, 1933–39

A totalitarian state?

In the aftermath of the Second World War, the image of the Nazi state was of an efficient and highly organised system, run on strictly hierarchical lines, with all power concentrated in Hitler's hands. The Nazi state was viewed as totalitarian – it had total control over all aspects of society, and was organised to reflect Hitler's will, which was the basis for law after the Enabling Act was passed.

A chaotic state?

Since the 1960s, however, this interpretation of Hitler's power and the working of the Nazi state has been challenged by historical evidence suggesting that the organisation and decision-making processes of the state were in fact chaotic and inefficient. There were no clear decision-making procedures, and often no clear lines of accountability.

Structures were often duplicated and overlapping in their functions, creating inefficiency. From 1936, for example, the Office of the Four Year Plan had created economic policy at the same time as the Economics Ministry retained responsibility for it. Several Nazi leaders were able to build up vast power, and often competed with one another for dominance. The Nazi party bureaucracy sometimes competed with the state institutions like government ministries and the independent *Gauleiter* who were only accountable to Hitler.

The nature and extent of Hitler's power

In the Nazi state, all decisions were supposed to emanate from Hitler. However, the chaotic state and Hitler's own haphazard methods of working meant that he did not always control decision-making and for this reason, some historians have questioned the idea that Hitler was an all-powerful dictator. Very few direct orders seemed to have come from Hitler, who only issued 34 decrees during his 12 years in power.

Where Hitler was particularly interested in policy, he did take a dominant role, however. In foreign policy, Hitler steered policy by first rejecting the Treaty of Versailles and then by developing expansionist plans. In 1936, Hitler took the decision to remilitarise the Rhineland against the advice of his generals, and he was instrumental in the process of *Anschluss* in 1938. It was Hitler's decision to push forward with an expansionist policy in Eastern Europe in the late 1930s.

'Working towards the *Führer*'

In other areas, while Hitler did not always make direct decisions, policy was developed which reflected his wishes. It has been argued that many people within the Nazi state took decisions by 'working towards the *Führer*' – that is, as Hitler's will was the source of law and authority and where there was an absence of a clear decision from Hitler, people sought to anticipate what Hitler would want and formulate policy on this basis. By this process, policy developed in the words of one Nazi bureaucrat, 'along the lines that the *Führer* would wish'.

Examples of 'working towards the *Führer*'

- Goering was prepared to enact Hitler's aim of a *Wehrwirtschaft*, war economy. He was given far-reaching powers by Hitler over economic policy as Head of the Office of the Four Year Plan in 1936. In contrast, Hjalmar Schacht, the Finance Minister, who had previously dominated economic policy, was sidelined after this time, as he did not want to devote the same level of resources to rearmament that Hitler wanted.
- Goebbels orchestrated *Kristallnacht* partly because he was out of favour with Hitler following an affair with a Czech actress (Czechs were considered racially inferior by Hitler). He attempted to win favour with Hitler by 'working towards' him.

⚠ Simple essay style

Below is a sample exam question. Use your own knowledge and the information on the opposite page to produce a plan for this question. Choose four general points, and provide three pieces of specific information to support each general point.

Once you have planned your essay, write the introduction and conclusion for the essay. The introduction should list the points to be discussed in the essay. The conclusion should summarise the key points and justify which point was the most important.

> How accurate is it to say that, in the years 1933–39, Germany was a totalitarian state under Hitler's complete control?

ⓘ Recommended reading

Below is a list of suggested further reading on the topic of the Nazi state.
- Ian Kershaw, 'Working Towards the Führer – Reflections on the Nature of the Hitler Dictatorship' in *The Third Reich*, Christian Leitz (ed.) (1999), pages 231–52
- Richard J. Evans, *The Third Reich in Power* (2006), pages 20–81
- Ian Kershaw, *The Nazi Dictatorship – Problems and Perspectives of Interpretation* (new edition, 2015), pages 81–108

Support for the Nazi regime

A consensus dictatorship?

Historians have debated whether the Nazi system was one based on popular support – a consensus dictatorship – or whether, in fact, the Nazi regime's power rested on repression and terror.

Evidence that the regime was popular

There were no significant attempts to overthrow the regime in the 1930s and underground opposition did not have widespread support during this era. Historian Robert Gellately has argued that the regime can be said to be a 'consensus dictatorship' because it relied so heavily on collaboration from ordinary people who were supportive of the Nazi regime. A series of plebiscites that were held in Nazi Germany tend to indicate that people supported Hitler's policies, although their results were not reliable and they were not free or fair votes.

Date	Plebiscite question	% in favour
1934	Do you endorse Hitler taking over Hindenburg's remaining powers on Hindenburg's death?	90%
1936	Do you support the remilitarisation of the Rhineland?	99%
1938	Do you support the union of Germany and Austria (Anschluss)?	99%

Reasons for support for the regime

Why would people support a system with such abhorrent values?
- Perceptions of the Weimar years were very negative. The Nazi regime seemed to bring greater stability to the lives of many Germans.
- Some Nazi policies, such as foreign policy, may have been popular and some of their policies did improve the lives of some Germans. Unemployment fell and economic growth resumed by 1935. Some Nazi social policies also improved the standard of living for certain groups of people. Non-Jewish pregnant women were given free health care, for example.
- The propaganda that people were subjected to may have been effective. A Ministry of Popular Enlightenment and Propaganda led by Joseph Goebbels had been established in 1933, and after this Goebbels worked hard to create an image of Hitler as a saviour of Germany. The annual Nuremberg Rally became a showcase for Nazi power. Censorship went alongside propaganda – newspaper editors were accountable to the Propaganda Ministry for what they published and the content of newsreels was controlled. Radio was used to propagate Nazi messages.

Support during wartime

Despite evidence that many Germans were not wholly in favour of the decision to go to war in 1939, early successes helped to bolster morale and support for the regime. However, particularly following the Battle of **Stalingrad** (1942–43), support declined and more opposition began to emerge.

A number of measures helped to maintain support for the regime early on in the war.
- Until 1944, rations were in excess of the minimum calories required, and extra rations were given at Christmas and for those in strenuous jobs.
- Early victories in Poland, Norway, Denmark, Luxembourg, Belgium and France helped to maintain morale.
- Hitler resisted Albert Speer's calls later in the war to mobilise women. This may have helped morale.

Declining support

After 1942 evidence suggests that people were sometimes critical of Hitler and that non-conformity and cynicism were rife. Many people in the Hitler Youth were disaffected. Factors that caused support for the regime to weaken included the following.
- Working conditions were difficult – hours at work increased, particularly in armaments factories.
- Some young people reacted negatively to the militarisation of the Hitler Youth after 1939.
- Defeat at Stalingrad could not be covered up by the regime, as the scale of the losses was so great.
- Allied bombing of German cities seems to have weakened morale in some areas, such as in the Rhineland. In total, Allied bombing in Germany killed 305,000 people, injured 780,000 and destroyed 2 million homes.
- The Soviet advance from 1943 worried the German public, who feared Russian invasion.
- The 1944 rocket campaign against south eastern England and Allied ports like Antwerp failed to have a decisive impact on the course of the war and caused morale to decline.

Even at this stage, however, there was no widespread rebellion against Nazi rule.

Support your judgement

Below are a sample exam question and two basic judgements. Read the exam question and the two judgements. Support the judgement that you agree with most strongly by adding a reason that justifies the judgement.

> How far do you agree that Nazi propaganda was the main reason for widespread popular support for Hitler's regime in the years 1933–45?

The Nazi regime was supported by many people in Germany for a variety of reasons, and while propaganda helped to strengthen support, this was only one reason for it.
_____
_____

The support that many people had for the Nazi regime was a result of the Nazis' effective use of propaganda
_____
_____

Tip: whichever option you choose, you will have to weigh up both sides of the argument. You could use phrases such as 'whereas' or words like 'although' in order to help the process of evaluation.

Turning assertion into argument

Below are a sample exam question and a series of assertions. Read the exam question and then add a justification to each of the assertions to turn it into an argument.

> How accurate is it to say that the Nazi regime enjoyed widespread support in the years 1933–45?

The plebiscites held in the Germany in the 1930s may indicate that the regime enjoyed support because
_____
_____

Collaboration with the regime was widespread, which shows that
_____
_____

Opposition to the Nazi regime was limited in the period 1933–45 which suggests that
_____
_____

Edexcel AS/A-level History Germany and West Germany 1918–89

Opposition and dissent

Was the regime really popular?

Some historians have opposed the idea that the Nazi state was a consensus dictatorship. Some evidence from **SOPADE**, the **Gestapo** and **Sicherheitsdienst** (the SS's secret police, the SD) reports indicates that people did not always wholeheartedly support the regime. Furthermore, the level of opposition increased after 1942, when Germany began to struggle in the war.

Opposition, non-conformity and resistance

Some evidence suggests that civil disobedience and non-conformity to Nazi ideals, such as listening to jazz, were common. Different methods of opposition include:
- active resistance – such as attempts to overthrow the regime
- protest – such as criticism of an aspect of Nazi policy
- non-conformity – failure to adhere to Nazi ideals.

There was very little active resistance, a little protest and significant levels of non-conformity in Nazi Germany. People did not always pull together in a unified *Volksgemeinschaft* in quite the way that the Nazis wished, but neither did many people want to actually get rid of the regime.

Opposition groups

The Edelweiss Pirates

The Edelweiss Pirates were youth groups that were explicitly anti-Nazi. They wore banned uniforms and attacked the Hitler Youth while also holding their own activities for young people. During the Second World War, some members engaged in illegal activities such as sabotage.

The Swing Youth

The Swing Youth were non-conformists who listened to American jazz and dressed in an unconventional manner.

The Catholic Church

The Catholic Church continued to speak out where they felt their interests or values were threatened. In 1937, Catholic priests read out an encyclical from the Pope ('With Burning Concern') which condemned some Nazi ideas. In 1941 large protests against an order to remove crucifixes from Bavarian schools caused the order to be reversed. Bishop Galen attacked the **Aktion T4** 'euthanasia' programme and its existence was subsequently covered up. Galen was placed under house arrest.

Protestant churchmen

Individual Protestant churchmen attacked the regime. Dietrich Bonhoeffer spoke out against the regime and was arrested in 1943 and executed in 1945.

The White Rose

The White Rose student group was formed in Munich in 1942. The movement urged Germans to reject Nazi values on ethical grounds and reject the destructive path that the Nazis were following. The group distributed anti-Nazi letters and leaflets. Brother and sister Hans and Sophie Scholl were beheaded for their activities in the movement in 1943.

Left-wing resistance

There was some active underground resistance on the left, as hidden groups engaged in sabotage and created underground networks of safehouses and information. In the summer of 1941 there were 89 resistance cells in factories in Berlin. There were also communist groups in Hamburg and Mannheim and various active socialist groups, such as Red Patrol. The communist network, the Red Orchestra (*Rote Kappelle*), collected intelligence and engaged in the distribution of anti-Nazi leaflets. The network was uncovered and destroyed by the military intelligence in 1942.

Conservative resistance

A number of conservative opposition groups formed to seek a restoration of the rule of law and an end to the war. The Kreisau Circle was a conservative group led by *Junker* Helmuth Graf von Moltke. By the end of the war the group had contacts with the left-wing opposition and opponents of the regime in the army.

Resistance in the army

After Stalingrad, some army officers rejected the regime and sought to overthrow it. In the 1944 Bomb Plot, an army group tried to assassinate Hitler and seize power. Assassin von Stauffenberg's bomb did not kill Hitler, however, and the plot was uncovered. In total, 22 generals were executed and Field Marshall Rommel was prevailed upon to commit suicide.

Support or challenge?

Below is a sample exam question which asks how far you agree with a specific statement. Below that is a series of general statements which are relevant to the question. Using your own knowledge and the information on the opposite page, decide whether these statements support or challenge the statement in the question and tick the appropriate box.

How far do you agree that there was very little opposition to the Nazis between 1934 and 1945?

	Support	Challenge
Active resistance to the Nazi regime was rare in the 1930s		
Non-conformity and dissent were relatively widespread		
There were some instances of protest against Nazi policies		
SOPADE reports suggest a high level of support for Hitler		
There were some opposition groups, such as the Edelweiss Pirates and left-wing underground networks		
The Bomb Plot was an attempt to overthrow the Nazi regime in 1944		

Complete the paragraph

Below are a sample exam question and a paragraph written in answer to this question. The paragraph contains a point and specific examples, but lacks a concluding analytical link back to the question. Complete the paragraph, adding this link in the space provided.

How far do you agree that there was very little opposition to the Nazis between 1934 and 1945?

Active opposition to the Nazi regime was minimal, particularly in the 1930s, and there is evidence from the secret reports of the Social Democratic Party that Hitler and some of his policies were popular. There were no concerted attempts to overthrow the regime at this time, and examples of public protest were rare. However, there were some public protests, such as the occasion in 1937 when Catholic priests read out an encyclical by the Pope, 'With Burning Concern', which condemned some Nazi ideas. Furthermore, there were some opposition groups, such as the Edelweiss Pirates and the communist Red Orchestra, although the membership of such groups was very small. In addition, lower-level opposition was much more common, as many people failed to conform to Nazi ideals and complained about Nazi policies. Overall, in the 1930s

_____

_____

_____

Edexcel AS/A-level History Germany and West Germany 1918–89

Terror and repression

REVISED

It could be argued that historians who focus on the idea of a 'consensus dictatorship' understate the scale of the terror. One reason for the lack of opposition to the Nazis was the scale of brutal repression launched in the period of their consolidation in 1933–34 when 100,000 people were held in camps. In June 1934, terror was also used against some potential right-wing opponents of the regime during and after the Night of the Long Knives.

The terror state

There were many impediments to people resisting the Nazis:
- The Nazis established a system of concentration camps to house undesirable elements.
- The Nazis ran an extensive network of terror and repression. From 1936, the head of the *Schutzstaffel* (SS), Heinrich Himmler, was in charge of a huge security network including the SS, security service, the police and the security police (including the Gestapo).
- The courts were used to suppress opposition in the mid-1930s. In 1935, 5,000 people were convicted for high treason, the prison population increased by 53,000 and 23,000 inmates of prisons were classed as political prisoners.
- People had no civil rights or freedom: the Reichstag Fire Decree (see page 38) removed the Weimar constitution's protections in this area. People lost the rights to freedom of speech and freedom of assembly and so had little power to organise any kind of opposition. The Gestapo could arrest and hold people in custody for any reason or none, while a law of 24 April 1933 made beheading the penalty for seeking to reduce Hitler's power.
- The Gestapo may have been small in number, but their network of informants made it hard for people to speak out. The regime kept an eye on people via agents such as party officials and Block Wardens who monitored their local areas for signs of deviancy.
- People were not free to express discontent or opposition to the Nazis in the plebiscites of the 1930s, which were conducted in an atmosphere of intimidation.
- *Gleichschaltung* meant that the Nazis were in control of most aspects of the state and that people who might potentially oppose them had been removed. So, for example, in April 1933 the Law for the Restoration of the Civil Service purged the civil service, and all trade unions were abolished on 1 May 1933, replaced with a Nazi organisation, the DAF. In July 1933, all other political parties were abolished.

Was the Nazi state a consensus dictatorship?

It is difficult to sustain the argument that the Nazi state was fully a consensus dictatorship, given that people so completely lacked freedom and were subject to terror and propaganda. The lack of active opposition may be accounted for by the success of the initial Nazi efforts to smash their political opponents. There is also evidence that non-conformity and civil disobedience were widespread.

However, evidence also seems to suggest that there were high levels of support for Hitler personally and that many people credited the Nazis with certain successes.

The picture that emerges is complex. Levels of support may have varied at different times, and equally an individual may have collaborated at certain points, while objecting to Nazi policies on other occasions. Non-conformity is difficult to interpret. Its widespread existence supports the idea that the Nazis did not succeed in completely controlling the population. Expressions of non-conformity did not necessarily indicate that a person was completely opposed to the existence of the Nazi regime, however.

Spot the mistake

Below are a sample exam question and a paragraph written in answer to this question. Why does this paragraph not get into Level 4? Once you have identified the mistake, rewrite the paragraph so that it displays the qualities of Level 4. The mark scheme on page 113 will help you.

> How far do you agree that the Nazi regime relied entirely upon terror to maintain its control in the years 1933–45?

> The Nazi regime relied to a significant extent on terror in the 1930s. The Nazis established a system of concentration camps to house undesirable elements. They also ran an extensive network of terror and repression. From 1936, the head of the Schutzstaffel (SS), Heinrich Himmler, was in charge of a huge security network including the SS, security service, the police and the security police (including the Gestapo). Block Wardens monitored people in their local areas for signs of deviancy. Furthermore, the courts were used to suppress opposition in the mid-1930s. In 1935, 5,000 people were convicted for high treason, the prison population increased by 53,000 and 23,000 inmates of prisons were classed as political prisoners. In addition, people had no civil rights or freedom: the Reichstag Fire Decree removed the Weimar constitution's protections in this area.

Support or challenge?

Below is a sample exam question which asks how far you agree with a specific statement. Below that is a series of general statements which are relevant to the question. Using your own knowledge and the information provided on the opposite page, decide whether these statements support or challenge the statement in the question and tick the appropriate box.

> How far do you agree that the Nazi regime relied mainly upon popular support for its power in the years 1933–45?

	Support	Challenge
In 1935, 5,000 people in Germany were convicted of high treason		
100,000 people were held in concentration camps by the Nazis after they gained power		
Block Wardens monitored people on behalf of the Nazi party		
The Gestapo often relied on denunciations from the public		
There is evidence that many Nazi policies were popular		

Nazi racial policies

Origins
Europe had a long history of Christian anti-Semitic attacks on Jewish communities, known as pogroms. While in most parts of Europe the **Enlightenment** period had seen improvements in the rights of Jews, in certain areas, such as Tsarist Russia, Jews remained oppressed and pogroms occasionally still occurred. At the turn of the twentieth century, old prejudices against Jews fused with new pseudo-scientific racial ideas (see page 20) and the idea that the Jews were racially inferior began to influence anti-Semitic extremists.

Nazi racial policies
Racial ideas were at the heart of everything that the Nazis did. They aimed to create a 'racially pure' **master race** in an expanded and dominant Germany. The 'racial' strength of Aryan Germans was viewed as the key to establishing a strong Germany. Groups seen as harmful to German racial strength were classed as 'outsiders' and subject to persecution. In Nazi Germany, the doctrine of Aryan racial supremacy had dangerous consequences for Jews and other people who did not fit into the Nazis' conception of a master race. The ultimate result was genocide and mass murder during the Second World War.

Persecution of Jews in Europe – timeline

Year	Persecution affecting Jews
1933	1 April – boycott of Jewish shops
	April – all Jews except war veterans removed from the civil service
1935	September – The Nuremburg Laws banned 'intermarriage'; Jews removed from German citizenship
1938	March – Violent attacks on Jews and Jewish property following *Anschluss*; 45,000 Austrian Jews forced to emigrate
	November – *Kristallnacht*: anti-Jewish attacks on thousands of businesses and synagogues; 25,000 Jewish men sent to concentration camps
	Aryanisation began; Jewish property seized; Jews banned from German economic life
1939	January – Reich Central Office for Emigration established to promote emigration of Jews out of Europe

Policies towards other outsider groups
Other groups who were considered 'outsider' groups and excluded on 'racial' grounds from the *Volksgemeinschaft* included:
- Gypsies (Roma and Sinti) – this group was the first to be murdered because of 'racial' identity. When the Second World War broke out, German Gypsies were deported to Poland. In 1940, a group of Roma children at Buchenwald was the first to be gassed in a concentration camp.
- Disabled people – the Nazis wanted only people that they classed as 'racially fit' in the Third Reich, and the 1933 Law for the Prevention of Hereditarily Diseased Offspring permitted compulsory sterilisation for those with hereditary conditions. In 1939, the Aktion T4 scheme was launched, in which disabled babies and children were murdered.
- Homosexuals – gay people were subject to Nazi persecution partly because they were viewed as resisting the Nazi desire for all Aryans to breed. In 1936, a Reich Central Office for the Combating of Homosexuality was established. Approximately 15,000 German gay people were imprisoned.

In addition, from the mid-1930s the Nazis' political enemies and **asocials** (people who did not conform to Nazi social ideals) were often imprisoned in concentration camps, including the homeless and alcoholics.

Mind map

Use the information on the opposite page to add detail to the mind map below.

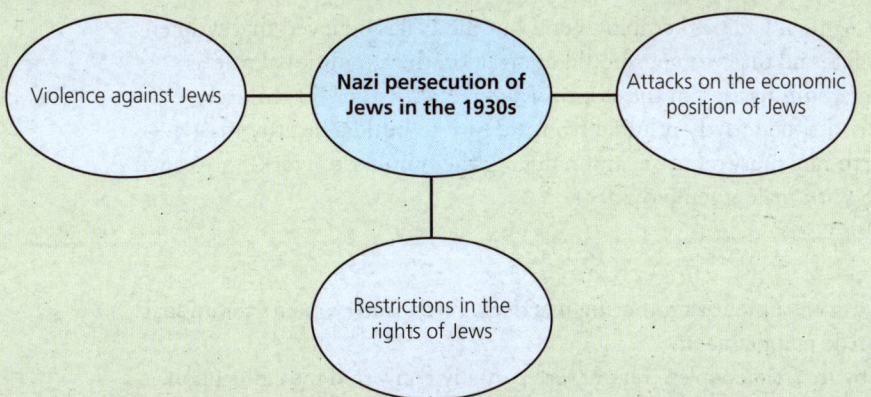

- **Nazi persecution of Jews in the 1930s**
  - Violence against Jews
  - Attacks on the economic position of Jews
  - Restrictions in the rights of Jews

Develop the detail

Below are a sample exam question and a paragraph written in answer to this question. The paragraph contains a limited amount of detail. Annotate the paragraph to add detail to the answer.

> How far do you agree that Nazi policies towards Jews became ever more extreme in the years 1933–45?

To a significant extent, Nazi policies towards Jews became more extreme over time. When the party first came to power Hitler was fairly cautious in pursuing his more ideological and extreme ideas. Despite this, measures were taken in 1933 to prevent Jewish people from working within the government. Nazi policy became more extreme in 1935, when steps were taken to restrict marriages between Jews and non-Jews, and to define who was Jewish and exclude these people from citizenship. The year of the Berlin Olympics, 1936, saw Nazi policies and discrimination towards Jewish people reduce, as the Party tried to create a positive impression internationally. In this sense, Nazi policies towards Jewish people did not increase at this point. However, in 1938 persecution increased again, as Jewish property was increasingly confiscated, and during Kristallnacht there was widespread and orchestrated violence against Jewish people, property and synagogues, and mass arrests of Jewish men.

Nazi policies towards women

REVISED

Nazi ideas about women

In Weimar Germany many women had paid employment, but the Nazis believed that women should not work. Nazi officials said that women should focus upon their traditional role as homemakers and childbearers, summarised in the slogan '*Kinder, Küche, Kirche*' ('children, kitchen, church'). The Nazis' attitude partly resulted from a desire to build a healthy master race – it was felt that the birth rate must increase, and reducing the number of working women would, it was believed, help with male unemployment.

Nazi policies

Nazi policies towards women were aimed at promoting marriage, births and women's traditional roles (and, thus, reducing female employment).

- Loans could be obtained by married couples. These were partially converted into gifts upon the birth of each child.
- Maternity benefits and family allowances were improved, and taxes were reduced for those with children.
- Contraception advice was restricted and anti-abortion laws enforced.
- Propaganda promoted idealised images of mothers, and honorary crosses were awarded to those with large families (a gold cross was awarded for having eight children).
- To reduce female employment, women were banned from working in many professional industries, such as medicine and law. Women who left employment to get married could obtain an interest-free loan of 600 Rentenmarks. Propaganda campaigns encouraged women to leave employment and employers to favour men.
- Women were restricted to only 10 per cent of university places.

The results of Nazi policies towards women

The results of Nazi policies in this area were mixed. The birth rate rose from 14.7 per 1,000 Germans in 1933 to 20.3 per 1,000 in 1939 and the proportion of women in the labour force decreased from 37 per cent in 1933 to 33 per cent in 1939. However, more women actually worked, as the labour force in Germany expanded at during this time – rapid rearmament was not really feasible without female labour. Measures to restrict female employment affected small numbers of middle-class, educated women. Additionally, the rate of marriages did not increase significantly during the 1930s. Where the Nazis achieved their aims (for example, in a rising birth rate) it is difficult to establish whether this was due to their policies or other factors, such as rising prosperity which encouraged more people to have children.

Nazi women's organisations

Women were barred from most areas of the Nazi party ruling structures, but could participate in the National Socialist Womanhood (NSF) and the German Women's Enterprise (DFW). These organisations were not really designed to encourage female participation in politics, however – they existed to promote Nazi ideology regarding women's role.

Support or challenge?

Below is a sample exam question which asks how far you agree with a specific statement. Below that is a series of general statements which are relevant to the question. Using your own knowledge and the information on the opposite page, decide whether these statements support or challenge the statement in the question and tick the appropriate box.

How far do you agree that the role of women in Germany in the years 1919–39 changed completely as a result of Nazi policies?

	Support	Challenge
Some young women in Weimar Germany lived independent, self-supporting lives		
The Nazis discouraged women from working and restricted women's places at university to 10 per cent		
The Nazis encouraged and incentivised women to stay at home and have children		
The number of women working increased during the 1930s		
Most women had a traditional role within the family during the Weimar era		
Women were banned from many professional occupations during the Nazi era		

Turning assertion into argument

Below are a sample exam question and a series of assertions. Read the exam question and then add a justification to each of the assertions to turn it into an argument.

How far do you agree that the position of women in Germany between 1919 and 1939 changed completely as a result of Nazi policies?

It was harder for women to live independent lives in Germany at the time of the Nazis because

The position of professional women in Germany changed as a result of Nazi policies because

The working lives of women in Germany was not completely altered by Nazi policies as

Nazi policies may have affected women's role as mothers in that

Nazi education and cultural policies

Nazi ideas about children and education

For the Nazis, children were central to providing the future 'master race'. The Nazis felt that children could be indoctrinated with Nazi ideas, education should be harnessed to serve the state and Nazi ideology and that children should be conscripted to build the movement and to provide future soldiers and mothers.

Nazi educational policies

Jewish teachers and teachers considered to be politically dubious were removed from their jobs in 1933. Remaining teachers were encouraged to join a Nazi Teachers' League, and could be sent on retraining schemes to educate them in Nazi ideas on education. The curriculum was altered to reflect Nazi values, including a nationalist version of German history and, in biology, a focus on Nazi racial ideas, such as racial hierarchy and **eugenics**. The educational curriculum was also used to reinforce traditional gender roles, with boys encouraged to participate in tough physical training and girls undertaking classes in cookery.

Nazi youth organisations

Youth organisations were designed to indoctrinate children in Nazi ideology and train them for their roles in Nazi Germany.
- The Hitler Youth (HJ) was formed in 1926. The HJ offered activities such as hiking and camping and also, increasingly, military training. Membership was made compulsory in March 1939. The increasing militarisation of the HJ reduced its popularity during the Second World War.
- The League of German Maidens (BDM) organised sporting activities and camping trips as well as training girls in their role as future homemakers. During the war, members of the BDM volunteered to help with charity collections and in hospitals. Later, BDM members were involved in anti-aircraft activities (attacks from the ground on enemy aircraft).

The impact of Nazi policies towards children and education

Nazi educational policies caused a decline of educational standards, partly because the curriculum had been affected by ideology and partly because the regime emphasised physical fitness rather than intellectual success. Evidence suggests that discipline in schools declined. Nazi youth organisations did provide children with expanded opportunities to participate in sport and social activities and travel in the German countryside, and the organisations were popular. However, the increasingly compulsory and regimented nature of Nazi youth organisations alienated some who had initially been attracted to the Nazis when they had represented a rebellion against established values. Some young people were actively involved in groups that rejected Nazism, most notably the Edelweiss Pirates.

Nazi cultural policies

Hitler was an enthusiast for certain types of art and architecture but saw culture as a means to promote Nazi ideas. Under the Nazis, modern art was denounced as degenerate and artistic endeavours were encouraged that promoted Nazi racial ideals. Books by Jewish authors or those considered to promote communist, liberal or other non-Nazi ideas were often banned or even burned, as in Berlin in May 1933. The artistic developments of the Weimar era were denounced. Hitler encouraged the development of **grand** schemes of classical architecture, such as those designed by Albert Speer. Architecture was supposed to embody the strength and the triumph of the Nazi movement.

Complete the paragraph

Below are a sample exam question and a paragraph written in answer to this question. The paragraph contains a point and specific examples, but lacks a concluding analytical link back to the question. Complete the paragraph, adding this link in the space provided.

How far did were children in Germany subject to indoctrination between 1933 and 1945?

Children in Nazi Germany were subject to indoctrination to a significant extent. This occurred at school and in propaganda directed at children by the Nazi regime through youth organisations, such as the Hitler Youth and the BDM. At school, the curriculum was altered to reflect Nazi ideas and to influence children. In biology, for example, Nazi racial ideas and Nazi ideas about the role and position of men and women were taught. In the Hitler Youth, membership of which became compulsory in 1939, boys were taught militaristic values, while girls in the BDM were trained in the role as homemakers. In these ways,

_____

_____

Establish criteria

Below is a sample exam question which requires you to make a judgement. The key term in the question has been underlined. Defining the meaning of the key term can help you establish criteria that you can use to make a judgement.

Read the question, define the key term and then set out two or three criteria based on the key term which you can use to reach and justify a judgement.

How accurate is it to say that the lives of children in Germany <u>changed completely</u> between the years 1919 and 1945?

Definition:

_____

_____

Criteria:

_____

_____

_____

Nazi economic policies, 1933–39

The German economy in 1933

Germany's economy was still in serious trouble when the Nazis took over: the economy had shrunk by around 40 per cent, and it is estimated that 8 million people were unemployed.

Schacht, Mefo bills and the New Plan

Banker Hjalmar Schacht was the dominant figure in Nazi economic policy 1933–36. His policies built upon work started during the von Papen and von Schleicher governments, and Schacht focused upon job creation and stimulating economic growth through use of government policies and expenditure.

- Public investment tripled and government spending increased by 70 per cent between 1933 and 1936.
- The Reich Labour Service employed 19–25-year-olds.
- Public works schemes saw the construction of *autobahns*, houses and public buildings.
- Armaments schemes also provided employment, as did agricultural schemes such as land reclamation projects.

These measures were paid for partly from taxation, but Schacht also designed the Mefo bills scheme to finance government spending. Mefo bills were essentially government IOUs which could be used to pay for spending and then exchanged within five years for real money. Mefo bills earned 4 per cent interest every year.

In his economic plan, the **New Plan** (September 1934), Schacht also tried to encourage German trade by establishing trading agreements with other countries such as Romania.

The results of all these policies were quite successful: unemployment fell and production increased by around 90 per cent between 1932 and 1936, but one problem that Schacht had not managed to solve was balance of payments – Germany imported more than it exported, leaving it short of foreign currency.

Goering, *Wehrwirtschaft* and the Four Year Plan

Despite Schacht's success, by 1936 he was falling out of favour with Hitler. With unemployment reduced and the economy growing once more, Hitler wished to focus policies upon his main concern of building a fearsome military machine. Hitler now wanted the economy to become one geared up for a major war, a *Wehrwirtschaft*. Schacht wished to focus economic policy more on developing exports to address the balance of payments problem. In August 1936, Hitler resolved this disagreement by giving Hermann Goering sweeping powers over the economy as Plenipotentiary of the Four Year Plan. Hitler wanted Germany to be ready to fight a major war within four years and Goering was prepared to enact policies to achieve this.

The Four Year Plan, 1936

- In order to fight a large war, it was felt that Germany needed to be **autarkic**, or economically self-sufficient. Therefore, the plan involved increased production in agriculture and raw materials and the production of ersatz (substitute) materials, such as artificial rubber, to replace imports. These were not always of good quality.
- Massive expansion of armaments was planned – a huge industrial enterprise, Reichswerke Hermann Goering (RWHG), was established in Salzgitter to develop armaments production.

The Four Year Plan was partially successful. Massive rearmament occurred and in some areas (for example, explosives) huge expansion was achieved, but autarky was not attained. By 1939, a third of raw materials were still imports, and targets were not achieved.

Living standards 1933–39

Farmers

By 1933, agriculture in Germany had been in depression for a number of years. In addition to the work of the **Reich Food Estate**, which regulated agricultural production and consumption, measures were also taken to protect small- and medium-sized farms. Grants were provided for improvements to farms, debt repayments reduced, and tariffs on imported food were increased. Initially, these measures improved the standard of living of German farmers, whose incomes increased by 41 per cent between 1933 and 1936. Agricultural wages still lagged behind urban wages, however, and from 1937 farm incomes stagnated again. A labour shortage severely hit farms and the industry struggled with rising labour costs.

Workers

The effect of Nazi policies on the standard of living for workers was mixed. Job creation schemes helped to reduce unemployment and some of the Nazis' benefit programmes improved working families' standards of living, but incomes in real terms declined and working hours increased. Some Nazi social policies also improved the standard of living for certain groups of people. Non-Jewish pregnant women were given free health care and by 1938, 2.5 million families enjoyed increased benefits for larger families.

> ## Simple essay style
>
> Below is a sample exam question. Use your own knowledge and the information on the opposite page to produce a plan for this question. Choose four general points, and provide three pieces of specific information to support each general point.
>
> Once you have planned your essay, write the introduction and conclusion for the essay. The introduction should list the points to be discussed in the essay. The conclusion should summarise the key points and justify which point was the most important.
>
>> How far do you agree that Nazi economic policies in the years 1933–39 brought few significant benefits to the German people?

> ## Spectrum of importance
>
> Below are a sample exam question and a list of general points which could be used to answer the question. Use your own knowledge and the information on the opposite page to reach a judgement about the importance of these general points to the question posed.
>
> Write numbers on the spectrum below to indicate their relative importance. Having done this, write a brief justification of your placement, explaining why some of these factors are more important than others. The resulting diagram could form the basis of part of an essay plan for a section of the essay that focuses on the period 1933–39.
>
>> How far do you agree that economic policies in Germany were effective between 1933 and 1945?
>
> 1. Agricultural incomes increased in 1933–37 but stagnated after 1937
> 2. Production in Germany almost doubled in the early years of Nazi rule
> 3. Unemployment reduced dramatically in the early years of Nazi rule
> 4. The Nazis struggled to achieve autarky
> 5. Ersatz materials were sometimes of poor quality
>
> ←——————————————————————————→
> Least important   Most important

Government in wartime

During the war, the chaotic tendencies of Nazi government increased as Hitler withdrew even further from direct control of much of the government. The most ideological part of the regime, the SS, became increasingly powerful and radical during the war.

Governmental anarchy

The structure of government continued to lack clear decision-making procedure and lines of accountability, and contained complex and overlapping structures. The economic requirements of the war created a new layer of complexity, as bodies such as the Todt organisation and the SS pursued their own economic agendas. **Factionalism** grew as ministries, the party and other organisations, such as the army and the SS, vied for power.

The role of Hitler

Hitler was primarily focused upon military matters during the war, and did not generally concern himself with other areas of government. His secretary Martin Bormann often acted to deny other people's access to Hitler. Himmler did visit Hitler to discuss the Holocaust, however. Hitler considered himself a military expert, but his interference in areas such as the war with the Soviet Union were not generally constructive. He also trusted Goering's decision-making, for example in relation to the **Battle of Britain** and supply lines on the Eastern Front. However, Goering's judgements on these issues turned out to be flawed.

As the war continued, the high rate of casualties on the Eastern Front damaged morale and provoked criticism of Hitler, who was by this point rarely seen in public – from 1943 Goebbels was much more the public face of the regime. Following the German defeat at Stalingrad, Goebbels gave and then publicised a speech at the *Sportpalast* arena in Berlin, calling for all Germans to support an effort for 'total war'. It was also Goebbels who orchestrated the response to the 1944 Bomb Plot, and who arranged rapidly for Hitler to give a speech on the radio, demonstrating that he had survived and was not badly injured.

The role of the SS

The lawlessness of the Third Reich increased during the war. The SS were entrusted with running Nazi-occupied territories in Eastern Europe, and instituted brutal and exploitative policies in these areas. By 1944, the organisation's army, the *Waffen SS* (which was separate from the rest of the German army, the *Wehrmacht*), contained 900,000 people responsible for the most extreme aspects of Nazi policy – the mass killings of European Jews and the system of death camps.

Support your judgement

Below are a sample exam question and two basic judgements. Read the exam question and the two judgements. Support the judgement that you agree with most strongly by adding a reason that justifies the judgement.

How accurate is it to say that government in Germany was characterised by chaos between the years 1933 and 1945?

> Government in Germany was strongly chaotic during the Second World War.
> _____
> _____

> Government in Germany could not be said to be wholly chaotic during the Second World War.
> _____
> _____

Tip: whichever option you choose, you will have to weigh up both sides of the argument. You could use phrases such as 'whereas' or words like 'although' in order to help the process of evaluation.

Develop the detail

Below are a sample exam question and a paragraph written in answer to this question. The paragraph contains a limited amount of detail. Annotate the paragraph to add additional detail to the answer.

How far do you agree that Hitler was a weak dictator in the years 1933–45?

> During the Second World War, in many ways Hitler appeared to be a weak dictator, as he withdrew further from decisions. The chaos of the Nazi state actually increased during the war, and Goebbels was often the more public face of the regime. Powerful individuals sometimes struggled to meet with Hitler and decision-making remained chaotic. However, during this period Hitler did take a strong interest in military decisions, and in these areas could not be said to be a weak dictator. Furthermore, those who exercised great power, such as Goering, Goebbels and Himmler, only did so on Hitler's authority. As during the 1930s, during the war Hitler continued to intervene more directly and show his powers in areas that he thought were most important, such as military matters.

The war economy

The German economy, 1939–41

Early on in the war, Hitler sought to dramatically expand the German war economy. Between 1939 and 1941, German military expenditure doubled. By 1941, 55 per cent of the workforce was involved in projects related to the war. Despite these efforts, German productivity was disappointing and below that of its enemies. Britain produced twice as many aircraft as Germany in 1941 and the USSR produced 2,600 more tanks. The chaotic organisation of the Nazi state hindered economic efficiency, as the various bodies responsible did not co-ordinate effectively. During the war, the Office of the Four Year Plan, various parts of the SS, the Ministry of Economics, the Ministry of Armaments and the armed forces all had responsibility for armaments production, while at a local level, the powerful *Gauleiters* often interfered with economic plans.

The appointment of Speer, 1942

To try to resolve these difficulties, Fritz Todt, Head of the Ministry of Armaments, simplified the production of armaments in January 1942. Industry was now directed to increase productivity. Hitler sought to further improve matters by appointing his trusted confidant Albert Speer as Minister of Munitions in February 1942, following Todt's death. In September 1943, Speer's powers were extended when he was given responsibility for all industry and raw materials as Minister for Armaments and Production. Speer took a number of actions, including:

- developing the work of Todt in establishing a Central Planning Board to coordinate economic organisation while also giving industry more freedom to develop
- trying to exclude the military from economic planning
- encouraging the employment of women
- using concentration camp prisoners as labour
- preventing the conscription of skilled workers
- deploying production lines
- encouraging the standardisation of armaments and establishing an Armaments Commission to oversee this.

Speer had considerable success as ammunition production rose by 97 per cent, tank production rose by 25 per cent and total arms production by 59 per cent. Between 1942 and 1944 German war production trebled. Raw materials were also used more efficiently and productivity per munitions worker increased by 60 per cent.

The failures of the war economy

Although German production levels increased, Germany was still out-produced by the USA and, crucially, by the Soviet Union. In the end, despite the improvements in efficiency that Speer had put in place, the war economy contributed to Germany's defeat. There are a number of reasons for this.

- The state remained chaotic, with some *Gauleiter* and the SS often acting against economic efficiency.
- Labour shortages held the economy back.
- Unlike in the Soviet Union, Britain and the US, women were not fully mobilised in the war effort.
- There was a heavy reliance on foreign workers (of whom there were 6.4 million by 1942). These were often little more than badly treated and underfed slave labourers: as a result their productivity was 60–80 per cent lower than that of the average German worker.
- Shortages of raw materials such as coal and oil held the German economy back – the production of ersatz materials did not fully compensate for this.
- The Germans needed the raw materials of the countries that they conquered in order to fight a major war, but the destructive manner of their conquest was not conducive to the effective exploitation of these resources.
- Supply of some materials such as iron ore and magnesium did improve as other countries were overrun but in the Soviet Union, Stalin's scorched earth policy of destroying infrastructure and useful supplies hindered the Nazis – in the Donbass region of the Ukraine in 1942, the output of coal mines was only 5 per cent of its pre-war levels.
- Allied bombing reduced the capacity of the German economy to expand further – industry was targeted and the Germans had to divert crucial resources towards defensive measures.

Turning assertion into argument

Below are a sample exam question and a series of assertions. Read the exam question and then add a justification to each of the assertions to turn it into an argument.

To what extent did German economic policy fulfil its aims between 1933 and 1945?

During the Second World War, German productivity was disappointing and below that of their enemies. Britain produced twice as many aircraft as Germany in 1941 and the USSR produced 2,600 more tanks. This meant that

_____
_____

Under the leadership of Albert Speer from 1942, ammunition production in Germany rose by 97 per cent, tank production rose by 25 per cent and total arms production by 59 per cent, which helped German war aims in that

_____
_____

The production of ersatz materials did not compensate for shortages of raw materials during the Second World War. This was a problem for economic policy because

_____
_____

The destructive policies followed by Nazi invaders in Eastern Europe hindered economic policy aims in that

_____
_____

Develop the detail

Below are a sample exam question and a paragraph written in answer to this question. The paragraph contains a limited amount of detail. Annotate the paragraph to add detail to the answer.

To what extent did German economic policy fulfil its aims between 1933 and 1945?

During the Second World War, the Nazis only achieved their economic aims to a limited extent. Production levels remained disappointing in Germany and at a lower level than that of their enemies. Albert Speer did have some success from 1942 at improving this situation, but it was not sufficient to gain an advantage against, for example, the Soviet Union. One issue was that the labour was not always productive: the Nazis relied on forced foreign workers, who were less efficient, and they did not mobilise women in the workforce to the same extent as the Soviets. Furthermore, the Nazis did not manage to avoid shortages of materials during the Second World War, despite invading many other countries possessing raw materials.

The domestic impact of the war

REVISED

The impact of the war on ordinary Germans was profound, although the problems with shortages were not as bad as those seen during the First World War. The war affected different social groups in different ways.

The impact on workers

- In order to try to maximise the productivity of German workers, wages were reduced and bonuses and extra overtime payments were banned at the start of the war. This strategy backfired, however, as there was then a higher level of absenteeism. Consequently, by October 1939, wage levels were restored.
- The regime also now sought to improve its mobilisation of labour by transferring workers in non-essential work to war work and by creating a register of men and women of working age.
- As the war dragged on into 1944, the impact on German workers became severe, as holidays were banned and the working week was increased to 60 hours per week. Workers were in a weak position to resist these new pressures.
- Workers were also kept in line via the system of organising them into groups overseen by a loyal party member.

The impact on women

- Married women with young children were often left alone to manage food and fuel shortages and look after the home as men were conscripted.
- Nazi ideology emphasised the role of women as mothers and homemakers and thus the regime was left with a dilemma when there were labour shortages. Hitler refused to authorise the mass conscription of women, however, and even though the power to conscript women existed, it was not much used.
- Women did not voluntarily join the workforce in large numbers as families of conscripted men received reasonable benefits. The numbers of women employed in industry actually decreased between 1939 and 1941.
- The demands of total war required an adjustment in Nazi policy towards women. From January 1943, all women between 17 and 45 were required to register to work, although there were exemptions for pregnant women, those with two or more children and the wives of farmers, who were seen as essential to maintaining agricultural production. Necessity had forced Hitler to modify, though not entirely abandon, his policies towards women.
- In the later stages of the war, Hitler was persuaded to increase the upper age limit of women compelled to work to 50 and there was a significant increase in the number of women workers. By 1945, 60 per cent of workers were women and women undertook some military duties, such as anti-aircraft operations.

Women workers

Nazi ideology and policy had encouraged women to stay at home and raise children. Despite this, 52 per cent of German women worked at the time of the outbreak of war. The combination of the failure to actually conscript women or organise a campaign to increase their participation, combined with the already fairly high level of female employment, meant that increasing the labour supply via the use of women workers did not really occur.

Mind map

Use the information on the opposite page to add details to the mind map below.

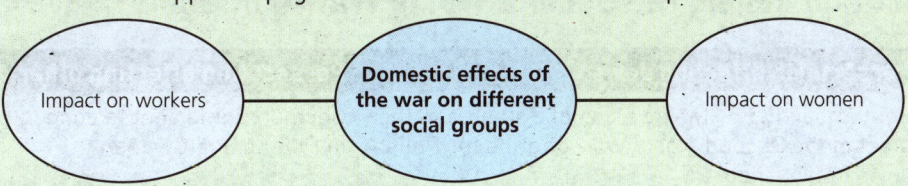

- Impact on workers — **Domestic effects of the war on different social groups** — Impact on women

Delete as applicable

Below are a sample exam question and a paragraph written in answer to this question. Read the paragraph and decide which of the possible options (in bold) is most appropriate. Delete the least appropriate options and complete the paragraph by justifying your selection.

How far did the position of women in Germany change 1933–45?

The position of women in Germany during the Second World War changed to **a small/some/a substantial** extent. Women's role as homemakers and mothers was to a large extent maintained, and because of his ideology, Hitler refused to authorise the mass conscription of women. Even though the power to conscript women existed, it was not much used. Furthermore, women did not voluntarily join the workforce in large numbers as families of conscripted men received reasonable benefits, and the numbers of women employed in industry actually decreased between 1939 and 1941. During wartime many women did experience a change to their role, however, as they were left without their husbands and had to become the head of the household. In addition, eventually, more women did get involved in the workforce, as the demands of total war required an adjustment in Nazi policy towards women, and from January 1943 all women between 17 and 45 were required to register to work, although there were exemptions. By 1945, 60 per cent of workers were women and women undertook some military duties such as anti-aircraft operations. Overall, during the Second World War, the position of women in Germany changed **slightly/moderately/entirely**

_____
_____

The 'Final Solution' and the Holocaust

REVISED

Nazi persecution during the Second World War – timeline

Year	Persecution affecting Jews	Persecution affecting other groups
1939	September 1939 – the invasion of Poland and the start of the Second World War; ghettos for Polish Jews established October – German Jews placed under curfew	German Roma sent to concentration camps in Poland and Germany October – the 'euthanasia' programme against disabled children starts
1940	The Madagascar Plan drawn up – a plan to move 4 million European Jews to live in Madagascar, an idea eventually abandoned as impractical	A group of Roma children were gassed in Buchenwald concentration camp Start of the murder of 70,000 mentally ill people
1941	All Jews forced to wear the Star of David June – following the invasion of the Soviet Union, *Einsatzgruppen* and their local supporters carried out systematic massacres of Jews	
1942	January – The Wannsee Conference: representatives of various party and state organisation agreed to the 'Final Solution' Spring – death camps established at Auschwitz, Sobibor and Treblinka	
1943–44	Transportation of Jews from all over Europe to death camps	

The role of Hitler

Hitler's speeches and writings showed that anti-Semitism was fundamental to his world-view. His ideas were the inspiration behind the ever-escalating anti-Semitism of his regime. It is also inconceivable that Hitler did not agree to the policy of the 'Final Solution' and indeed a diary entry of Himmler's indicates that at a meeting to discuss the 'final solution of the Jewish question' in December 1941, Hitler authorised or ordered that Jews should be 'exterminated as partisans'. Most historians do not believe that Hitler had a clear plan for the 'Final Solution' that pre-dated the war, however.

Cumulative radicalisation and the chaotic state

Another part of the explanation for the 'Final Solution' is that it was a consequence of the process of ever-growing extremism that occurred in the Third Reich as a result of the chaotic decision-making procedures. The chaos encouraged local initiatives and ideological radicalism. Cumulative radicalisation led to escalating action – German Jews were subject to restrictions and repression at the start of the war, but were not confined to ghettos. Polish Jews were then subject to the same measures and ordered into overcrowded ghettos run by the SS. When Germany invaded the Soviet Union, *Einsatzgruppen*, following the army to ensure SS control, had wide-ranging instructions to eliminate opponents, and massacres of Jews followed. These became systematic as the army moved eastwards and culminated in a policy of organised genocide in the death camp system.

The impact of the war

The 'Final Solution' developed in the context of war.
- The German invasion of Poland had created what the Nazis regarded as a problem. The Jewish population of Poland was large, at around 3 million. Jews were forced into ghettos, which were overcrowded and insanitary. When Jews from other parts of Europe started to be deported to the ghettos the problem intensified.
- Fighting, particularly on the Eastern Front, was brutal and dehumanising and made it easier to consider extreme action.
- When invading areas of the Soviet Union, *Einsatzgruppen* carried out the first systematic massacres of the Holocaust. When the 'Final Solution' was planned, mass killings of Jews and some other groups such as Roma were already occurring in the USSR.
- As the invasion of the Soviet Union put strains on the German war economy, the cost of feeding people in ghettos was considered too great.
- With the failure of the Madagascar Plan and the success of small-scale experiments with murder by gas, the plan for the 'Final Solution' was drawn up and executed – the systematic transportation to death camps of the entire Jewish population of Europe.

Quick quizzes at www.hoddereducation.co.uk/myrevisionnotes

Complete the paragraph

Below are a sample exam question and a paragraph written in answer to this question. The paragraph contains a point and specific examples, but lacks a concluding analytical link back to the question. Complete the paragraph, adding this link in the space provided.

> How far do you agree that Nazi racial policy became ever more extreme between the years 1933 and 1945?

In general, Nazi racial policy became ever more extreme during the time they were in power, and this was particularly true during the Second World War. The invasion of Poland saw the creation of ghettos in that country, and intensification of anti-Semitic measures. The Nazis deported other Jewish populations to their ghettos when they invaded further territories, which caused a deterioration of conditions in the ghettos. Furthermore, during the invasion of the Soviet Union from June 1941, Nazi killing squads, assisted by local collaborators, systematically murdered Jewish and Roma populations in these areas. Mobile gas chambers (which had previously been used by the Nazis to murder some disabled people) were then deployed, before the plan began to be enacted from late 1942 to establish death camps and transport remaining European Jews and Roma to these camps. During the Second World War, Nazi racial policies became more radical and

_____

_____

Recommended reading

Below is a list of suggested further reading on the topic of the Holocaust.
- David Cesarani, *The Final Solution – The Fate of the Jews 1933–49* (2016), pages 451–580
- Nikolaus Wachsmann, *KL – A History of the Nazi Concentration Camps* (2015)

Exam focus

REVISED

Below is a Level 5 answer to an A-level exam-style question. Read it and the comments around it.

How far do you agree that the Nazi regime relied mainly upon popular support for its power 1933–45?

The Nazi regime relied to some extent upon popular support for its power between 1933 and 1945, but I do not agree that it relied mainly upon this. The Nazis also relied to a significant extent upon the use of terror and the suspension of civil rights to maintain their power.

To some extent, the Nazi regime depended upon popular support to keep power between 1933 and 1945. They had come to power as the most popular political party in Germany, having won the largest vote share in the July and November 1932 elections at which they gained 37 per cent and 32 per cent of the vote. In the March 1933 election, after they had taken power, the party increased their vote share to 44 per cent. The party had also become a popular mass movement by 1933, with a large membership, a network of membership organisations such as the Hitler Youth, and mass rallies. It is very unlikely that the Nazis would have come into power in the first place without the popularity that they had. Furthermore, the party continued to believe, at least in the 1930s, that it was important to be seen to win popular votes. In a series of plebiscites held throughout the 1930s, the German people voted (or appeared to vote) in favour of Nazi policies, such as the remilitarisation of the Rhineland. These votes show that the Nazi Party wished to continue to demonstrate that it had popular support for its actions.

Specific evidence is used to support the point.

The Nazi Party also showed that their power relied upon popular support through their extensive use of propaganda. The Nazis used modern propaganda methods in their elections campaigns before they came to power, for example during the 'Hitler over Germany' campaign of 1932 during the presidential elections. They continued to rely upon these methods once in power, which indicates that the party placed great emphasis upon the value of popular support. In power, Goebbels became head of a Ministry for Popular Enlightenment and Propaganda and great efforts were put into publicising Nazi policies in a positive way, into promoting Nazi ideas and into promoting the idea of Hitler as the saviour of Germany. During the Second World War, Goebbels continued to focus on propaganda to try and maintain morale, for example, during his 'total war' speech. These propaganda efforts, along with some successes in foreign and economic policy, may have helped to increase support for the Nazi regime. Support for Hitler was widespread and evidence suggests that people were supportive of some of the foreign policy successes, such as rearmament and remilitarisation of the Rhineland. In addition, some ordinary people sometimes benefitted from Nazi policies, such as full employment policies and family benefits. All of these policies show that the Nazis sought popular support, and at least to some extent relied upon it.

Quick quizzes at www.hoddereducation.co.uk/myrevisionnotes

However, the Nazis did not rely mainly on popular support for their power as they also relied to a significant extent upon terror. In the initial period after they came to power, the Nazis attempted to eliminate their main opponents. After the Reichstag Fire, civil rights were suspended and people could be arrested for any reason or none. Around 100,000 people, mainly socialists, communists and trade unionists, were put into concentration camps at this time – Dachau, the first of these camps, was opened in March 1933. Hundreds of newspapers were closed down. In May 1933 the entire trade union movement of Germany was shut down and replaced by a Nazi organisation, and in July all other political parties were banned. The courts were used to try people accused of treason, which essentially meant opposing the Nazi Party. Those who did not fit into the Nazis' *Volksgemeinschaft* were isolated and oppressed in Germany. The Jewish community, for example, saw their rights eroded in the Nuremberg Laws in 1935, had property forcibly removed and suffered violence and terror during *Kristallnacht* in 1938. During the Second World War, opponents to the regime often faced even harsher penalties, as can be seen in the execution of the members of the White Rose movement in 1944. At this time the Nazis increased their persecution of their enemies, up to and including mass murder and genocide. Overall, the Nazis were able to maintain power partly through weakening or destroying their opponents, isolating and ultimately trying to destroy those who did not fit into their racial ideal, and through creating widespread fear and intimidation.

The candidate returns at the end of the paragraph to make their argument.

In conclusion, the Nazi regime relied upon popular support to an extent to maintain their power, but also to a significant extent on terror and intimidation. People were not free to protest or oppose the regime, and faced very harsh penalties if they attempted to resist. However, the regime clearly felt that popular support was important for maintaining their power, and put great efforts into propaganda. In addition, some of their policies were popular, and they did enjoy significant popular support. Overall, it was a mixed strategy of propaganda and terror.

A clear answer to the question.

This is a high-level response as the candidate gives a clear but balanced answer to the question. There is a great deal of supporting evidence deployed and a clear conclusion that explains the argument being given.

Find the evidence

The most important element in producing an argument is supporting evidence and examples. Read the essay again and identify where evidence has been used effectively to support a point.

AS-level questions

Was the Night of the Long Knives the main reason for the growth of Nazi power within government in the years 1933–39? Explain your answer.

To what extent were there changes in the role of women in the years 1919–45?

3 Historical interpretations: How far was Hitler's foreign policy responsible for the Second World War?

The influence of German history on Nazi foreign policy

REVISED

The historical debate

In many ways, the causes of the Second World War can seem simple: Hitler's ideology and aggression led the world to a conflict of appalling destructiveness. However, most historians argue that there were other causes of the Second World War. In order to understand them, it is necessary to consider:
- the influence of German history on Nazi foreign policy
- Hitler's ideas and his role in the shaping of Nazi foreign policy
- the reasons for the German invasion of Poland in 1939
- the contribution of other nations to the outbreak of war.

The influence of German history

Some historians have argued that Germany's modern development had followed a special path (in German, *Sonderweg*) that caused the country to be more militaristic and aggressive than other developed nations. Historians who hold this view point to the authoritarianism and militarism of German culture, the fact that the Second Reich was created after a series of military conflicts and the influence of the militaristic traditions of the Prussian Army on German culture. According to this argument, these are the long-term causes of the war.

Nazi policy and German history

There are undoubtedly some ways in which Nazi foreign policy reflected previous German policy or attitudes.
- The 'September Program', drawn up by the German government at the start of the First World War, set out Germany's ambition to take over vast areas of Europe.
- In some respects, Kaiser Wilhelm II's *Weltpolitik* scheme of colonial expansion, prior to 1914, might also be regarded as a kind of forerunner of Hitler's ambitions. Moreover, *Weltpolitik* was based on racist assumptions.
- The idea that the German people needed territorial *Lebensraum*, 'living space', to expand into, had grown in popularity in Germany in the late nineteenth century. Indeed, the desire to conquer territory in Eastern Europe and Russian was popular prior to 1914.
- Anti-Semitism, and other kinds of racism, had a long history in Germany, and in the late nineteenth century, pseudo-scientific ideas about 'racial purity' were common.
- The idea that all German peoples should be united in one country was also held by some pre-war Germany and some German-speakers in the Austro-Hungarian Empire.

Critics of this this view

Even though there were similarities between Nazi policies and some earlier policies and ideas, there are many historians who reject the notion that Germany had a *Sonderweg*. Critics argue that most other major European countries were imperialist and racist in the nineteenth and early twentieth centuries, and yet this did not lead them to prepare for a major European war during the 1930s.

Franco–German tensions and the Treaty of Versailles

Some historians have argued that long-term relations between France and Germany led to the outbreak of the Second World War. The Second Reich was formed in the aftermath of the defeat of France in the Franco–Prussian War of 1870–71. At the end of this conflict, the new German Reich took over the French regions of Alsace-Lorraine. French resentment about German aggression and suspicions about German actions continued throughout the period 1871–1914. After the end of the First World War, the French were determined to get their territory back and also to ensure that Germany would never humiliate France again.

Conclusions: German history and Nazi foreign policy

Most historians would accept that the ideas of right-wing German and Austrian nationalists, such as the unity of all Germans and *Lebensraum*, did influence Nazi ideas. However, how far these issues were the main cause of the Second World War is disputed.

Contrasting interpretations

Below are sample Section C exam questions and the accompanying extracts. The extracts offer different interpretations of the issue raised by the question. Identify the interpretation offered in each extract and complete the table below, indicating how far the extracts agree with each other, and explaining your answer.

	Extent of agreement	Justification
Extracts 1 and 2		

In the light of differing interpretations, how convincing do you find the view that 'Hitler's restless quest for empire' led to the outbreak of the Second World War?

To explain your answer, analyse and evaluate the material in both extracts, using your own knowledge of the issues.

Study Extracts 1 and 2. Historians have different views about how far Hitler's foreign policy was responsible for the Second World War. Analyse and evaluate the extracts and use your knowledge of the issues to explain your answer to the following question. How far do you agree with the view that it was Hitler's aggressive foreign policy which led to the outbreak of war in 1939? **AS**

EXTRACT 1

From Richard Overy, The Origins of the Second World War, *published 2016.*

The Second World War once seemed a simple event to explain. If it did not exactly boil down to one word – 'Hitler' – the war was nevertheless the Germans' war. Without Hitler's restless quest for empire, war might have been avoided.

In practice, the outbreak of war was a great deal more complicated than this. Historians cannot even agree on the pressures that pushed Hitler towards war. While some see a clear intention in his part to launch wars of aggression based on the ideas of racial struggle and world empire, others emphasise the importance of fear of domestic unrest and economic crisis brought about by the excessive cost of rearmament.

Arguments such as these mask a more important problem in explaining the outbreak of war. By concentrating on Germany we are in danger of forgetting that Germany was part, and quite a small part, of a global international structure. German statesmen reacted to problems over which, in many cases, they had no control.

EXTRACT 2

From David Olusoga and Casper W. Erichsen, The Kaiser's Holocaust: Germany's Forgotten Genocide, *published 2010.*

Nazism as a political ideology emerged, half-formed and half-baked, from the primordial Volkisch soup of the Munich beer halls. In this early stage – between 1919 and 1923 – what is most striking about Nazism as an ideology was its unoriginality. Nazism's roots in Volkisch mysticism and nationalist politics of the Second Reich have encouraged some historians to look for a single figure from whom Hitler might have derived political inspiration. The fact is that Nazism was not so much invented as reassembled from the enormous array of traditional nationalist obsessions and the racial pseudo-sciences that had mushroomed in the last decades of the nineteenth century. The acute fear of encirclement by other European powers, a determined belief that Germany was chronically overcrowded and an unshakable suspicion that the nation was being denied her rightful place in the world – these were all concerns that exercised the Kaiser and his clique as much as the future Fuhrer and his party. The prejudices and neuroses of the Second Reich were passed down to Hitler and the Nazis like family silver.

Hitler's role in shaping foreign policy

REVISED

Many historians argue that Hitler's actions and ideas were a major cause of the Second World War. Hitler sought *Lebensraum* and wanted to overturn the Treaty of Versailles. In order to achieve this he expanded the Germany military, and annexed Austria and the whole of Czechoslovakia prior to the invasion of Poland. His vision was of a huge, 'racially pure' German state at the heart of Europe, supported by satellite states whose populations were enslaved.

Hitler was personally instrumental in pushing foreign and economic policy in a more aggressive direction that made war more likely. For example, it was Hitler's decision to redirect economic policy from 1936 towards preparing for a large-scale war (see page 54). Additionally, in 1936 he went ahead with the remilitarisation of the Rhineland, breaching the Treaty of Versailles, against the advice of his generals.

In 1938, Hitler and Goering were behind the decision to push forward with the annexation of Austria. Hitler also steered his military **generals** towards preparation for a major European war from 1938, and purged any generals who opposed him during the **Blomberg-Fritsch Affair**. Hitler was central to events in Czechoslovakia in 1938 and 1939, as well as the decision to invade Poland in 1939, which, unlike much of his previous foreign policy decisions, was not initially popular with German people.

Master planner or opportunist?

Historians disagree on the extent to which Hitler had a plan for war, or how far the path to war was the result of Hitler seizing opportunities.

Masterplan?

There is some evidence that Hitler had a plan for world domination. Hitler set out his foreign policy aims in many speeches and documents.
- The Nazi 25 Points programme published in 1920, demanded the abolition of the Treaty of Versailles and land for Germany to colonise.
- *Mein Kampf* set out Hitler's vision to create *Lebensraum* in Eastern Europe.
- Hitler's *Second Book*, written in 1928 and published after his death, set out his *Stufenplan*, a stage-by-stage programme which aimed to make Germany the world's dominant power.
- The Four Year Plan was introduced in 1936 in order to get Germany ready for war in the early 1940s.
- The Hossbach Memorandum, a record of Hitler's discussion with senior generals which took place in 1937, set out Hitler's vision for *Anschluss* and the destruction of Czechoslovakia by 1945.

It is clear that Hitler's writings and his goals influenced Nazi policy. However, while Hitler's aims were clear, some historians argue that his writings do not constitute a fully worked out plan. Moreover, Hitler never wrote of starting a world war in 1939.

Opportunist?

Other historians argue that Hitler tended to improvise, making the most of opportunities as they arose. For example, Hitler was unsure how Britain and France would respond to the remilitarisation of the Rhineland, but after they accepted it, Hitler's foreign policy became bolder.

Plan for peace?

Some historians argue that throughout the 1930s Hitler's main goal was to avoid war. From this point of view, Hitler's attempt to find excuses to justify expansion into Czechoslovakia and Poland, and his willingness to sign treaties with Britain and France and the USSR, can all be viewed as evidence that Hitler was keen to expand without starting a major war.

RAG – rate the interpretation

Below are a sample exam question and one of the extracts referred to in the question. Read the question, study the extract and, using three coloured pens, underline it in red, amber or green to show:
- **Red:** counter-arguments and counter-evidence provided by the extract
- **Amber:** evidence that supports this interpretation
- **Green:** the interpretation offered by the extract.

In the light of differing interpretations, how convincing do you find the view that Hitler's opportunism led to the outbreak of the Second World War?

EXTRACT 1

From A. J. P. Taylor, The Origins of the Second World War.

As it was, he became involved in the world of action; and here, I think, he exploited events far more than he followed coherent plans. He did not so much aim for war as expect it to happen. Hitler certainly directed his generals to prepare for war. But so did the British, and for that matter every other government. By 'plan' I understand something which is prepared and worked out in detail. In my sense Hitler never had a plan for *Lebensraum*. There was no study of the resources in the territories that were to be conquered; no definition even of what these territories were to be. There was no recruitment of a staff to carry out these 'plans', no survey of Germans who could be moved, let alone any enrolment. When large parts of Soviet Russia were conquered, the administrators of the conquered territories found themselves running round in circles, unable to get any directive whether they were to exterminate the existing populations or to exploit them, whether to treat them as friends or enemies. The abstract speculator turned out to be also a statesman on the make who did not consider beforehand what he would make or how. He got as far as he did because others did not know what to do with him. As supreme ruler of Germany, Hitler bears the greatest responsibility for acts of immeasurable evil: for the destruction of German democracy; for the concentration camps; and worse of all, for the extermination of peoples. His foreign policy was different.

Add your own knowledge

Using the extract from the last activity, write around the edge of the extract any relevant knowledge of your own that would help you answer the question.

Tips:
- You can add your own knowledge that supports *and challenges* the extract.
- You can also add new alternative arguments that challenge the interpretation offered by the extract.

The contribution of other nations to the outbreak of the war

While there is no doubt that Hitler and Germany played an important role in starting the Second World War, other nations also played a role. Indeed, Hitler had the opportunity and confidence to ignore the Treaty of Versailles and launch aggressive actions because the weakness of the international system. During the 1930s:
- the USA and the USSR largely stayed out of foreign affairs
- Britain and France were not in a strong position to try to uphold international order, as they both had economic problems after the Depression, and France was very unstable politically
- the League of Nations was ineffective; the League was supposed to work for peace, but lacked the unity and power to take decisive action over aggression. For example, it was unable to stop Italy's invasion of Abyssinia in 1936
- the events of the Spanish Civil War (1936–39), which was won by the nationalists and fascists, strengthened Germany's international position. It led to greater unity between Italy and Germany. At the same time, Britain and France maintained a position of neutrality during the civil war, which created the impression that they would not intervene to stop military aggression.

Appeasement

'**Appeasement**' is the name given to the British and French policy towards Germany from 1935 to the invasion of Czechoslovakia in March 1939. Appeasement means making concessions in order to avoid war. It often has the negative connotation of weakness and passivity in the face of aggression.

The causes of appeasement

Britain and France adopted a policy of appeasement for several reasons.
- Britain and France wanted to avoid war. In the context of the Depression and the aftermath of the First World War, the British and French public were keen to avoid another conflict, at least until 1939.
- Many in Britain believed that the Treaty of Versailles had been excessively harsh, and therefore supported Hitler's policies to reverse the terms of the Treaty.
- France experienced a series of political crisis in the 1930s. Therefore, the French government did not feel strong enough to take decisive action against Germany without British support.

The consequences of appeasement

From 1935 to 1938, Britain and France were prepared to allow Germany to breach the terms of the Treaty of Versailles and follow an ever more aggressive foreign policy.

In pursing the policy of appeasement, Britain and France often overlooked or even consented to aggressive acts by the Nazi government. Britain and France took no action to force German forces to withdraw after the remilitarisation of the Rhineland. Britain and France did not stop *Anschluss*. Furthermore, when Hitler threated Czechoslovakia in 1938, British Prime Minister Neville Chamberlain preferred to negotiate the Munich Agreement, an international agreement between Britain, France, Germany and Italy – which the Czech government had little option but to sign, and which allowed Germany to take over the Sudeten part of Czechoslovakia, rather than stand up to Hitler.

Was appeasement misguided?

Chamberlain, in particular, is often criticised for the policy of appeasement. But appeasement gave the British time to rearm and prepare to fight Hitler. Between the signing of the Munich Agreement and the start of the war a year later, Britain developed radar and expanded its rearmament program. Nevertheless, by creating the impression that they would not resist German aggression, appeasement encouraged Hitler to think that his aggression would succeed.

Lack of unity

Concerted action by the USSR, France and Britain might have prevented Hitler's attack on Poland, and therefore prevented the outbreak of war. However, the three countries could not work together.

Britain was reluctant to work with the USSR. British leaders did not want to share information and intelligence with a communist country. Suspicion of communism made an alliance impossible.

Challenge the historian

Below are a sample Section C exam question and one of the accompanying extracts. You must read the extract, identify the interpretation it offers and use your own knowledge to provide a counter-argument, challenging the extract's interpretation.

In the light of differing interpretations, how convincing do you find the view in Extract 1 that 'actions by other nations could have minimised the likelihood of the outbreak of war'?

Interpretation offered by the source:

_____
_____

Counter-argument:

_____
_____
_____
_____

EXTRACT 1

From Helen Roche, Interpretation, *published 2015.*

Was there ever a point at which other nations could realistically have called a halt to the Third Reich's expansionism? There did indeed exist such windows of missed historical opportunity, during which actions by other nations could have minimised the likelihood of the outbreak of war.

Foreign reactions to the remilitarisation of the Rhineland were to set the tone for all future dealings with Hitler; the annexation therefore constitutes a crucial turning point. The dictator himself apparently stated that 'the 48 hours after the march into the Rhineland were the most nerve-wracking of my life …' Indeed it would have been easy for the French army, then the largest in the world, to stop the German forces in their tracks. However, France insisted upon full British support. Both Prime Minister Baldwin and Chamberlain then insisted that the British public would refuse to countenance any risk of war.

In conclusion: had British and French politicians taken Hitler's ambitions more seriously and had Chamberlain not been so convinced that war with Germany must be prevented it might have been possible to subdue Germany before she had rearmed sufficiently to be a truly dangerous threat. Ultimately, however, foreign weaknesses only served to radicalise the dictator's resolve.

Why did Germany invade Poland in 1939?

The British, the French and the Polish Guarantee

Even though the British government sought to avoid war, they were not prepared to allow Germany to grow too powerful. With this in mind, following the German takeover of Czechoslovakia, the British and French government signed the Polish Guarantee in March 1939, in which they pledged to support Polish independence. French and British politicians hoped that this would persuade Hitler to stop German expansion. Indeed, in some ways the Polish Guarantee marked an end to the policy of appeasement.

Hitler and Poland

Hitler aimed to continue German expansion, while avoiding war with Britain and France. Crucially, Hitler did not take the Polish Guarantee seriously. He viewed the British and French governments as weak, and failed to realise that, after the Munich Agreement, Britain and France were determined to stop further German expansion. As a result, Hitler was prepared to ignore the Polish Guarantee and continue with his plans to invade Poland.

The Nazi–Soviet Pact

In August 1939 the USSR and Germany signed the Nazi–Soviet Pact. This allowed Poland to be divided between the USSR and the Germans. The pact meant that Germany could attack Poland without fear of Soviet opposition.

German invasion

Once the Nazi–Soviet Pact had removed the threat that the USSR might attack if Germany invaded Poland, Germany authorities faked an incident on the Polish-German border to provide a pretext for the invasion. On 1 September 1939, Germany commenced its attack.

Masterplan or miscalculation?

Historians disagree regarding how far the invasion of Poland was part of Hitler's masterplan to take Europe to war, or how far it was a miscalculation.

Many historians have argued that Hitler did not seek a large-scale conflict in 1939. From this point of view, either he assumed that Britain and France would back down, or he assumed that any conflict would be short-lived. Either way, many historians claim that Hitler did not want a European war.

Hitler's mistake?

Some historians claim that the policy of appeasement had convinced Hitler that Britain and France would not act against Germany. In this sense, they argue, Hitler misjudged the situation.

The British and French declaration of war

On the same day that Germany launched its invasion of Poland, the British and French ambassadors in Berlin issued an ultimatum, stating that if German troops did not withdraw from Poland, Britain and France would declare war against Germany. On the evening of 2 September 1939, Chamberlain told the House of Commons that he had received no response to his ultimatum, and on 3 September he announced in a radio broadcast to the public that 'this country is at war with Germany'. Within hours, the French government had also declared war.

Ultimately, Britain and France decided to try and prevent further Germany aggression and expansionism.

Write the question

The following extracts relate to the causes of the collapse of the Soviet Union. Having read the previous pages about the Soviet Union's collapse, write a Section C exam-style question to accompany the extracts.

Study Extracts 1 and 2. In the light of differing interpretations, how convincing do you find the view that

_____

_____

To explain your answer, analyse and evaluate the material in both extracts, using your own knowledge of the issues.

Study Extracts 1 and 2. Historians have different views about how far Hitler's foreign policy was responsible for the Second World War. Analyse and evaluate the extracts and use your knowledge of the issues to explain your answer to the following question. How far do you agree with the view that

_____

_____

EXTRACT 1

From Richard Overy with Andrew Wheatcroft, The Road to War, *published 1989.*

War was not inevitable in 1939. With Hitler at the helm war at some time almost certainly was. The problem that the majority of more moderate German nationalists faced in the 1930s was the difficulty of creating a domestic political environment that would restrain Hitler. The brutal methods which had revolutionised Germany in 1933 were institutionalised. As the regime became more confident, and repression more widespread and effective, the scope for the radical agenda of racism and war became fuller and more explosive. But what really permitted Hitler to go further, to 'accelerate the pace', was the fundamental weakness of the international structure into which he burst. The world order dominated by Britain and France could scarcely cope with colonial squabbles; a Germany lurching rapidly and unpredictably towards superpower status was quite beyond control. The radical nationalists and racists around Hitler could see this; they tied themselves to Hitler in the hope of profiting from the new German order. British and French power was swept aside in 1940; Soviet power was almost destroyed a year later. But the strength of the United States tipped the scales.

EXTRACT 2

From Richard J. Evans, The Third Reich in Power, 1933–39, *published 2005.*

War had been the objective of the Third Reich and its leaders from the moment they came to power in 1933. From that point up to the actual outbreak of hostilities in September 1939, they had focused relentlessly on preparing the nation for a conflict that would bring European, and eventually world, domination for Germany. The propaganda image of Hitler as the world statesman who had given back Germans pride in their country almost single-handedly did not, of course, entirely correspond to reality. Even in the area of foreign policy there were occasions, notably the annexation of Austria, where he had followed the lead of others (in this case Goering), or, as in the Munich crisis, been forced against his inclination to yield to international pressure. Others, notably Ribbentrop, had also wielded considerable influence on the decision-making process at key moments. Nevertheless, it had indeed been Hitler above all others who, sometimes encouraged by his immediate entourage, sometimes not, drove Germany down the road to war between 1933 and 1939. He laid down the broad parameters of policy and ideology for others to apply in detail. At crucial junctures he took personal command, often uncertainly and hesitantly at particular moments of crisis, but always pushing on towards his ultimate goal: war.

Domestic reasons for the German invasion of Poland

Economics and public opinion

Some historians claim that the invasion of Poland was brought about by economic and political pressure in Germany.

The impact of the Four Year Plan

The Four Year Plan, and rearmament more generally, had a negative impact on the German economy. Some historians argue that this pushed Germany to war.

- The need for raw materials to make weapons caused a balance of payments crisis. In 1939, Germany was forced to slow down its rearmament drive. Hitler believed that a solution to this was to gain more territory and in so doing take hold of more resources. This could have been one of Hitler's motives for eastern expansion, which in turn led to war.
- Rearmament also had a negative impact on German living standards. Devoting huge amounts of resources to rearmament meant that Germany did not have the resources to improve wages, and it meant that the supply of consumer goods and food became limited. This economic pressure created discontent. Some historians argue that Hitler needed to go to war to unite the country.

Blitzkrieg

Some historians argue that *Blitzkrieg* provided a solution to Hitler's economic and political troubles. According to this view, Hitler was prepared to launch a *Blitzkrieg*, a lightning war, with Poland. A quick war would have the benefit of uniting Germany behind the war effort, making the government popular after a quick victory, and allowing Germany to seize Polish resources.

The role of other individuals

Some historians argued that other senior Nazis also had a role in pushing Germany towards war.

Ribbentrop

Joachim von Ribbentrop was appointed as Foreign Minister by Hitler in 1938. Ribbentrop replaced Constantin von Neurath, a conservative who wanted a pragmatic foreign policy. In this sense, Ribbentrop's appointment removed an obstacle to the development of a more aggressive foreign policy. Ribbentrop also played a key role in negotiating the Nazi–Soviet Pact of August 1939, which led the way to the invasion of Poland.

Goering

Hermann Goering was responsible for creating and equipping the **Luftwaffe**. Moreover, as head of the Four Year Plan Organisation he was responsible for much of the rearmament of the later 1930s. In this sense, Goering helped lay the economic and military foundations for war. In 1938 Goering also advocated an aggressive approach to *Anschluss*, which emboldened Hitler's foreign policy.

Goering also hid the failures of the Four Year Plan and the weaknesses of the *Luftwaffe* from Hitler. In so doing he encouraged Hitler to think that Germany was ready for war. This may well have persuaded Hitler risk war over Poland in 1939.

The nature of German government

A final domestic reason which might explain was is the nature of Hitler's government. Cumulative radicalisation (see page 62) meant that over time, radical Nazis and radical policies came to dominate government. In terms of foreign policy this meant that policies became more aggressive as the 1930s went on.

At the same time, conservatives and pragmatists had no way of stopping Hitler taking risks, as the checks and balances of the Weimar Constitution were ignored. This allowed Hitler to pursue an aggressive foreign policy without any effective opposition within government.

> ## ⚠ Linking extracts
>
> Below are a sample Section C question and the two extracts to which it refers. In one colour, draw links between the extracts to show ways in which they agree about the reasons for the invasion of Poland. In another colour, draw links between the sources to show ways in which they disagree.
>
> Study Extracts 1 and 2. In the light of differing interpretations, how convincing do you find the view that the German invasion of Poland came about as a result of Hitler's exploitation of events, rather than 'precise coherent plans' (Extract 1)?
>
> Study Extracts 1 and 2. Historians have different views about how far Hitler's foreign policy was responsible for the Second World War. Analyse and evaluate the extracts and use your knowledge of the issues to explain your answer to the following question. How far do you agree with the view that Hitler's ambitions led to the invasion of Poland in 1939? **AS**

EXTRACT 1

From A. J. P. Taylor, The Origins of the Second World War, *published 1961.*

Hitler speculated a good deal about what he was doing. As it was, he became involved in the world of action, and here, I think, he exploited events far more than he followed precise coherent plans. When other countries thought that he was preparing aggressive war against them, Hitler was equally convinced that these others intended to prevent the restoration of Germany as an independent Great Power. His belief was not altogether unfounded. At any rate, the British and French governments have often been condemned for not undertaking a preventive war in good time.

Here is the key to the problem whether Hitler deliberately aimed at war. He did not so much aim at war as expect it to happen, unless he could evade it by some ingenious trick. I agree that there was no clear dividing line in his mind between political ingenuity and small wars, such as the attack on Poland. The one thing he did not plan was the great war often attributed to him.

EXTRACT 2

From A. Boxer, Appeasement, *published 1998.*

The destruction of the Czech state made it clear that Hitler's ambitions went beyond the unity of all Germans. He had also displayed contempt for the Munich Agreement. Most people in Britain were now convinced that war with Germany was only a matter of time. Chamberlain, however, remained hopeful that peace would be secured. He recognised that he would have to take a tougher line with Germany and that rearmament would have to be accelerated but hoped that British firmness would bring Hitler to his sense and make him willing to negotiate. Chamberlain was reluctant to take steps likely to provoke Hitler into anything rash.

Exam focus (A-level)

REVISED

Below is a sample high-level essay. Read the question and the accompanying extracts, as well as the essay and the comments around it.

In the light of differing interpretations, how convincing do you find the view that it was 'Hitler above all others who … drove Germany down the road to war between 1933 and 1939' (Extract 1)?

EXTRACT 1

From Richard J. Evans, The Third Reich in Power 1933–39, *published 2005*.

War had been the objective of the Third Reich and its leaders from the moment they came to power in 1933. From that point up to the actual outbreak of hostilities in September 1939, they had focused relentlessly on preparing the nation for a conflict that would bring European, and eventually world, domination for Germany. The propaganda image of Hitler as the world statesman who had given Germans pride in their country almost single handedly did not of course entirely correspond to reality. Even in the area of foreign policy there were occasions, notably the annexation of Austria, where he had followed the lead of others (in this case Goering), or, as in the Munich crisis, been forced against his inclination to yield to international pressure. Others, notably Ribbentrop, had also wielded considerable influence on the decision-making process at key moments. Nonetheless, it had indeed been Hitler above all others who, sometimes encouraged by his immediate entourage, sometimes not, drove Germany down the road to war between 1933 and 1939.

EXTRACT 2

From Tim Mason, 'Some thoughts on the Origins of the Second World War', *published 1971*.

The economic, social and political tensions within the Reich became steadily more acute after the summer of 1937. While it seems safe to say that Hitler understood very little of their technical content, it can be proved that he was informed of their existence and was aware of their gravity. If the existence in the winter of 1937-8 of a conscious connection in Hitler's mind between this general crisis and the need for a more dynamic foreign policy cannot yet be established, the relationship between these two factors may nonetheless be suggested. The only 'solution' open to the regime of the structural tensions and crisis … was more dictatorship and rearmament, then expansion, then war and terror, then plunder and enslavement. The stark ever present alternative was collapse and chaos … A war for the plunder of manpower and materials lay square in the dreadful logic of German economic development under National Socialist rule.

Extract 1 clearly answers that 'Hitler above all others' drove Germany to war. The extract argues that war had been a long-term aim of the Nazi government and that German leaders had been preparing for war since Hitler's appointment as Chancellor in 1933. Extract 2 puts forward a different view. Essentially, it argues that Hitler was forced to go to war by the growing economic and political crisis of the late 1930s. Therefore, while both extracts claim that Hitler played a role in the outbreak of war, Extract 1 sees war as a deliberate policy, whereas Extract 2 presents the invasion of Poland as a reaction to circumstances.

[The introduction summarises the interpretation of both extracts, contrasting them and showing an understanding of the basis of arguments offered by both authors.]

Extract 1 claims that Hitler prepared Germany for war over the entire course of his government. Evans claims that Hitler and his government had 'focused relentlessly on preparing the nation for a conflict'. This view can be supported by the evidence of Nazi ideology, which focused on the superiority of the Aryan race, and which therefore aimed at 'European, and eventually world, domination' for the master race. Hitler's ideology, including his goal of *Lebensraum*, and his desire to reverse the terms of the Treaty of Versailles, therefore established the goals of the Nazi government which led the nation to war.

[Here the essay integrates own knowledge.]

Extract 1 goes further, arguing that Hitler not only set the general direction of policy, he made key decisions that took Germany to war. There is certainly evidence to support this.

Hitler personally made the decision to remilitarise the Rhineland in 1936. Hitler was also responsible for setting up the Four Year Plan Organisation and briefing his military chief about future war, a meeting recorded in the Hossbach Memorandum of 1937.

However, Extract 2 gives a different perspective. It argues that war emerged from 'the dreadful logic of German economic development under National Socialist rule' rather than Hitler's long-term goals. Extract 2 argues that Hitler's economic policy created 'economic, social and political tensions' leading to a 'general crisis' in the winter of 1937-38. Some historians agree with this, pointing to growing unrest among German workers as their living standards dropped due to the focus on rearmament. War, according to Extract 2, was the 'only "solution" open to the regime' to the crisis created by rearmament. According to this view, Hitler initiated a 'war for the plunder', rather than a war for European and then world domination, as Extract 1 claims. Extract 2 implies that Hitler launched a limited war in Poland in 1939 simply to get more resources, rather than intending to start a major war.

> The essay uses own knowledge to discuss the arguments of both extracts.

There are problems, however, with Extract 2's argument. First, it says there was a 'crisis' and that unrest was grave. However, as Extract 1 points out, the Nazis had put a lot of effort into propaganda, presenting Hitler as 'the world statesman who had given Germans pride in their country'. Levels of support for Hitler in Germany were quite high during the 1930s, and the SS and Gestapo had proved successful at ending resistance – therefore Extract 2's argument that Germany was experiencing a crisis so grave that war was the only solution is not wholly plausible.

> The essay evaluates the argument of Extract 2 using own knowledge and evidence from Extract 1.

Extract 1 argues that Ribbentrop and Goering also played a role in taking Germany to war. Ribbentrop replaced Neurath as German Foreign Minister in 1938, leading to a radicalisation in foreign policy. Indeed, Ribbentrop negotiated the Nazi–Soviet Pact, which helped clear the way for an invasion of Poland. Goering, as Extract 1 notes, played a key role in *Anschluss*. He also headed the rearmament drive, mentioned in Extract 2. Goering also exaggerated the success of the rearmament drive and the readiness of the airforce, perhaps leading Hitler to overestimate Germany's ability to fight a war in 1939.

> This paragraph extends the range of the essay by considering the secondary argument in Extract 1.

While Ribbentrop and Goering were influential, as Extract 1 argues, it was Hitler, 'above all others', who set the course for war. Hitler initiated the rearmament drive that Goering headed, Hitler dismissed Neurath and appointed Ribbentrop, and it was Hitler who set out his vision of conquest to generals in 1937. Indeed, in many ways Ribbentrop and Goering were merely 'working toward' Hitler by finding ways to fulfil his vision.

> Here the essay uses own knowledge to evaluate the argument of Extract 1.

In conclusion, Extract 1 is right to argue that Hitler, more than any other, 'drove Germany down the road to war'. Extract 1 is also right that Hitler had been preparing for war since 1933, through setting up the rearmament program and through propaganda. Hitler had a long-standing commitment to restore German honour through military strength and he was prepared to gamble with war, as he did over the Rhineland in 1936. However, Extract 2 may hold the key to the kind of war Hitler anticipated in 1939 – a *blitzkrieg*, rather than a full-scale European war. After all, Hitler tended to believe that Britain and France were weak, and therefore may not have anticipated that war with Poland would lead to war across Europe. Nonetheless, Extract 2 gives too little emphasis to Hitler's role, and focuses too heavily on economic and political problems, because Hitler consistently made the most of circumstances, using them to achieve his goals.

> The conclusion makes a supported judgement about the argument of both extracts.

This essay achieves a mark in Level 5 as it interprets both extracts with confidence, and clearly understands of the basis of their interpretations. It also integrates evidence from own knowledge in order to presents a supported overall judgement on the views given in both extracts.

Exam focus (AS-level)

REVISED

Below is a sample high-level essay. Read the question and the accompanying extracts, as well as the essay and the comments around it.

Historians have different views about how far Hitler's foreign policy was responsible for the Second World War. Analyse and evaluate the extracts and use your knowledge of the issues to explain your answer to the following question.

How far do you agree with the view that 'Hitler's policies were responsible for the outbreak of war in 1939?'

EXTRACT 1

From Victoria Harris, Interpretation, *published 2015.*

Historians have tended to view Hitler's actions in 1939 as a realisation of Nazi ideology. Hitler did make his imperial plans very clear in *Mein Kampf*. The National Socialists' foreign policy was, from the outset, focused on incorporating all ethnic Germans into the greater Reich, as well as destroying Bolshevism during the move east in search of greater *Lebensraum*, or living space. Hitler was under no illusions that the quest for European dominance would require war.

Germany also engaged in a series of aggressive actions that destabilised the status quo after 1933. Germany left the League of Nations, started rapidly rearming, began offering military support to Franco and remilitarised the Rhineland. Historians have used this evidence to argue that Hitler's policies were responsible for the outbreak of war in 1939.

EXTRACT 2

From Andre Flint, Nationalism Dictatorship and Democracy in Twentieth Century Europe, *published 2015.*

Having reunited German-speaking people into the Third Reich with the *Anschluss* and the seizure of the Sudetenland, Hitler turned his attention to Poland.

Finally realising that Hitler was not simply seeking a fair territorial settlement for Germany, but wanted European domination, the Western democracies agreed to protect Poland from German attack. Historians debate how far Hitler truly wanted a global conflict at this point; some argue that he hoped that he would only have to fight a small scale local war.

Whatever his intentions, an attack on Poland was a massive gamble. The British had promised to fight to protect Polish independence. Yet for Hitler, convinced that the Allies would not risk war with Germany to defend Poland, it was a chance worth taking. Hitler's gamble did not pay off, the war became a global conflict.

The two extracts present different views about how far Hitler's foreign policy was responsible for the Second World War. Extract 1 argues that the war was caused by Hitler's policies, which were based on Nazi ideology, whereas Extract 2 argues that the war occurred due to Hitler's gamble over Poland.

[The introduction summarises and contrasts the key interpretations offered by both extracts.]

Extract 1 points to the aggressive policies that Hitler pursued. It argues that policies such as 'offering military support to Franco and remilitarised the Rhineland' led to war. In essence, these policies were aimed at overturning the Treaty of Versailles, which Hitler viewed as a 'dictat' which took away German's freedom. Hitler's policies were, according to Extract 1, based on 'Nazi ideology'. In the long term Hitler wanted to destroy Bolshevism, establish *Lebensraum* and unite all Aryans in one state. Extract 1 argues that these aggressive policies caused war because they led to conflict with neighbouring countries, which caused war.

[Here the essay integrates detailed own knowledge, using it to discuss the view given in Extract 1.]

However, Extract 2 points to the international context of the outbreak of war. Whereas Extract 1 argues that it was the ideological nature of Nazi policies that caused war, Extract 2 argues that war came about because of Hitler's willingness to take big risks. Extract 1 and 2 both indicate that, for a time other countries were prepared to tolerate Hitler's aggressive foreign policy. For example, the remilitarisation of the Rhineland, mentioned in Extract 1, took place in 1936, years before war took place. France had wanted to resist the remilitarisation, but Britain was prepared to accept Germany's breach of the Versailles Treaty. From 1936 to 1938 Britain was willing to compromise with Germany. This explains why 'the *Anschluss* and the seizure of the Sudetenland' mentioned in Extract 2, did not lead to war. However, the policy of appeasement ended after the Munich agreement. For Extract 2, this is crucial in explaining the outbreak of war. The Polish Guarantee of 1939 committed France and Britain to support Poland. Hitler did not take the Polish Guarantee seriously, but it made attacking Poland a gamble. It was Hitler's willingness to take risks, rather than the general direction of his policy, that led to war because the 'gamble did not pay off' and the invasion of Poland 'became a global conflict'.

This paragraph begins with by comparing the argument of Extract 1 with that of Extract 2.

While Extract 1 focuses on the ideological roots of Nazi policy, it also implies that Hitler's policy responded to events, as Extract 1 discusses Germany's 'military support to Franco', which was not part of Hitler's mission to create *Lebensraum* or a 'racially pure' Germany. Extract 2 also points to Hitler's pragmatic side, noting that in 1939 he may have wanted 'a small scale local war' that Germany could win, rather than a war of global conquest. Hitler's willingness to act pragmatically also undercuts Extract 1's argument about Hitler pursuing ideological policies that led to war, because it indicates that he was prepared to act pragmatically, rather than following an inflexible ideological policy that would inevitably lead to war.

Here the essay uses evidence from both extracts to evaluate the view given in Extract 1.

Overall, Hitler's policy alone cannot be the cause of war. His policy, as both extracts show, was broadly consistent — it always aimed at expansion. However, it was only in 1939 that this policy of expansion led to war. What changed was the reaction of Britain and France and Hitler's perception of the risk of war. In 1936 Hitler viewed the remilitarisation of the Rhineland as a huge risk. However, after Britain and France accepted it, he assumed that Britain and France were too weak and cowardly to stand up to Germany. Hitler interpreted Britain's willingness to accept the *Anschluss* and German domination of Czechoslovakia as further evidence that Britain and France would not stand up to Germany. Therefore, in 1939 Hitler was 'convinced that the Allies would not risk war with Germany to defend Poland'. This led him to gamble. However, in 1938 Britain's attitude had changed — Chamberlain was no longer willing to accept German expansion. Therefore, Hitler's policy of invading Poland did lead to war, as Extract 1 claims, but it was not the policy alone. Britain's policy had changed more than Hitler realised and, as Extract 2 argues, Hitler's gamble did not pay off and led to war.

The essay concludes with a well-supported overall judgement, which discusses the interpretations presented in both extracts.

This essay gets a mark in Level 4 as it analyses the interpretations of both extracts, integrating detailed own knowledge to reach a supported overall judgement about the interpretations of both extracts.

4 Democratic government in West Germany, 1945–89

Return to democratic government: the creation of the Federal Republic of Germany, 1945–49

REVISED

Defeat and occupation

At the Yalta Conference on the future of post-war Europe, the USSR, the USA and Britain agreed to divide Germany between four zones of occupation: the French in the west, by their border; the British in the north-west; the USSR in the east; the USA in the south. The capital city, Berlin, which lay deep inside the Soviet occupation zone, was also to be divided between the four powers. The **Potsdam Conference** (17 July–2 August 1945), held after the Nazis had been defeated, reaffirmed the decision to divide Germany.

The Yalta Conference

The Conference was held before the Second World War was over, but when the Allied powers were certain of victory. The conference was held between 4 and 11 February 1945 at Yalta in the Crimea. The three main decision-makers were Josef Stalin, leader of the USSR; US President Franklin D. Roosevelt; and British Prime Minister Winston Churchill. At the time of the Yalta Conference, the USSR's Red Army was only 40 miles away from Berlin and occupied a vast swathe of Eastern Europe. It was agreed at the conference that the pre-war borders of Poland would be moved westwards, with the Soviet Union permanently keeping the eastern part of the country. The Polish borders on the west were to be shifted into what had been German territory. It was decided that there would be free elections in Poland and in other Eastern European countries. However, it was also agreed that the USSR, which had been attacked by Germany via Eastern Europe, would have a 'sphere of influence' in Eastern Europe. Democratic elections were not likely to be compatible with this.

The beginnings of the Cold War

The period after the Second World War saw conflict develop between the victorious powers, as the Soviet Union worked to strengthen its influence in Eastern Europe and the United States sought to limit the expansion of communism in Europe and the world. The two superpowers were keen to ensure their power and security, and were divided by their conflicting ideologies.

Tensions came to a head over the occupation and government of Germany. In the eastern Soviet zone, a pro-Soviet communist government was established, while the authorities in the Western, anti-communist British, American and French occupied zones increasingly co-operated with one another. Tensions rose through the first half of 1948, as the Soviets increasingly disrupted travel to and from Berlin. In June 1948 the British, American and French zones unified their zones into what was called Trizonia. A new currency, the Deutschmark, was introduced in the Trizone, despite Soviet opposition.

The Berlin blockade

Stalin wished to secure Soviet dominance over the whole of Germany and doubted the commitment of the USA to remain as occupiers, particularly in Berlin. He also felt that the unification of the rest of Germany posed a threat to Soviet power. In response to the introduction of the new currency in the Trizone, Stalin launched the Berlin blockade on 24 June 1948. Land and water connections into non-Soviet West Berlin were cut off, and rail and road traffic into the city stopped. Water was suspended and on 25 June, food supplies were also ended. Stalin aimed to force Britain, America and France out of Berlin. In response, as air routes remained open and were subject to an international agreement that the Soviets respected, the Western Allies launched a massive airlift operation to keep West Berlin supplied. At its height, the Berlin Airlift saw a plane full of supplies reaching Berlin every 30 seconds.

Not wishing to provoke a war, the Soviets did not obstruct the airlift and on 12 May 1949, ended the blockade. The Berlin Blockade was the first open conflict of the **Cold War**.

The establishment of the Federal Republic of Germany

On 23 May 1949, shortly after the blockade had ended, the Trizone became the Federal Republic of Germany (FRG or West Germany). The country was no longer officially occupied, although a substantial Allied military presence remained. In October 1949, the German Democratic Republic (GDR or East Germany), under Soviet domination in the east, was announced. Germany was to be divided in this way for 41 years.

Mind map

Use the information on the opposite page to add detail to the mind map below.

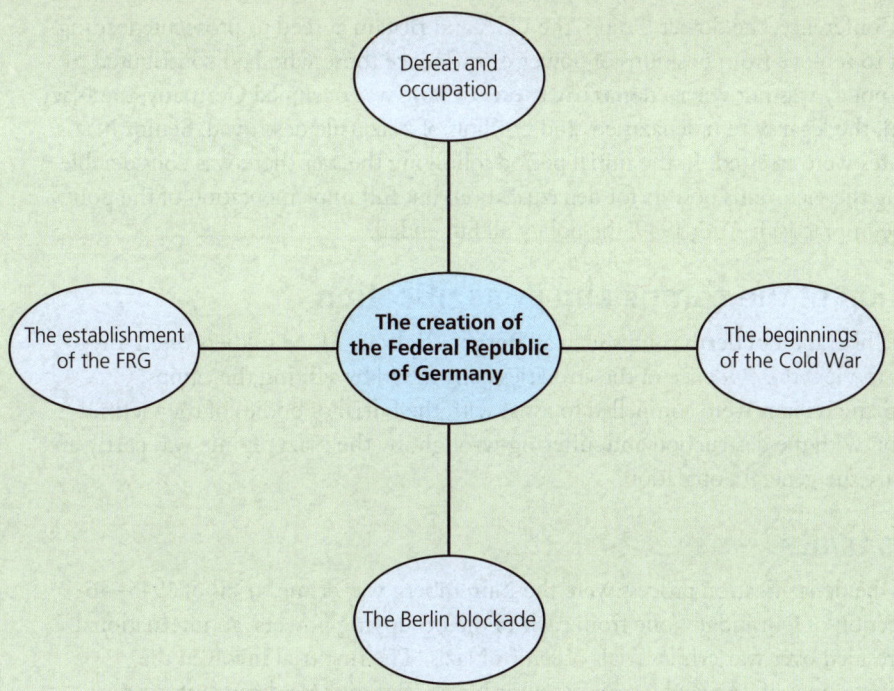

- Defeat and occupation
- The establishment of the FRG
- **The creation of the Federal Republic of Germany**
- The beginnings of the Cold War
- The Berlin blockade

Complete the paragraph

Below are a sample exam question and a paragraph written in answer to this question. The paragraph contains a point and specific examples, but lacks a concluding analytical link back to the question. Complete the paragraph adding this link in the space provided.

How far do you agree that the government of Germany was transformed in the years 1918–49?

German defeat in the Second World War and occupation by the Allies caused another transformation in the government of Germany. The Nazi dictatorship ended and power passed to the administrations of the four victorious powers: the USA, the Soviet Union, Britain and France. Not only was the country controlled by foreign powers, but also the government of Germany was transformed by the division of the country into four zones, one controlled by each of the four occupying powers. By 1949, the US, British and French zones had reunified, but the Soviet-controlled eastern section remained separate. Ultimately, one of the major transformations in the government of Germany that resulted from the Second World War was the creation of two separate Germanys at this time: a capitalist West Germany and a communist East Germany. In the western Trizone, steps were gradually taken to restore democracy to Germany — in this sense, the end of Nazi dictatorship was not so much a transformation but a restoration of parts of the Weimar system. Overall,

The denazification policies of the Western Allies, 1945–49

At the Potsdam Conference, the Soviet Union, the USA and Britain agreed to prosecute leading Nazis and sought to remove from positions of power or influence those who had contributed to the regime. This policy was known as '**denazification**'. In post-war occupied Germany, the Nazi Party was banned, the legal system denazified, and symbols of Nazi rule destroyed. Senior Nazis and military figures were arrested. In the initial period following the war there was considerable enthusiasm among the victorious powers for denazification, but full implementation of the policy was deemed to be impractical. After 1949, the policy all but ended.

The liberation of the camps and denazification

At the time of the liberation of death camps such as **Bergen-Belsen**, Allied soldiers often forced local populations to view the evidence of the atrocities committed by visiting the camps. Sometimes, German civilians were compelled to assist with the burial of bodies of the victims. This confrontation with the destruction and suffering wrought by the Nazi regime was partly an attempt to denazify the general population.

War crimes trials

A major focus of the denazification process were the Nuremberg war crimes trials of 1945–46. Under the jurisdiction of four judges (one from each of the occupying powers) an international criminal court presided over war crimes trials of senior Nazis. The first trial involved the prosecution for war crimes of 23 people, mainly senior Nazis. Ten of these defendants were executed, and Hermann Goering, who was sentenced to death, committed suicide the night before his execution. Several organisations, such as the Gestapo and the SS, were indicted and found to be 'criminal'. Further trials followed, including cases against judges and doctors who had been complicit with the regime.

The Nuremberg trials represented denazification in the sense of bringing some of those responsible for atrocities to justice, and it also provided a forum to present the evidence of Nazi criminality to the German public and wider world.

Cultural and educational denazification

Symbols of Nazi rule, such as the large swastika at the Nuremberg stadium, were destroyed. In education, efforts were made to retrain teachers (see page 52).

The limitations of denazification policies

Denazification did not continue after the election of **Konrad Adenauer** (see page 86) and in 1951 a law was passed calling the process in West Germany to a halt. By this stage, the Allies did not oppose this move.

Support or challenge?

Below is a sample exam question which asks how far you agree with a specific statement. Below that is a series of general statements which are relevant to the question. Using your own knowledge and the information on the opposite page, decide whether these statements support or challenge the statement in the question and tick the appropriate box.

How far do you agree that actions of the Allies were responsible for creating the stability of Federal Republic of Germany between 1949 and 1966?

	Support	Challenge
War crimes trials brought some senior Nazis to justice		
Denazification helped to reduce the appeal of Nazi ideas		
Defeat in the war caused disillusionment with Nazi ideas		
The Allies' denazification policy caused resentment among some Germans		
Denazification was a limited policy that left many people who had been active Nazis in positions of power and influence		

Recommended reading

Below is a list of suggested further reading on this topic.
- Frederick Taylor, *Exorcising Hitler – the Occupation and Denazification of Germany* (2011), pages 277–312
- Ann Tusa and John Tusa, *The Nuremberg Trials* (2003), pages 11–15
- Telford Taylor, *The Anatomy of the Nuremberg Trials – A Personal Memoir* (1992), Chapter 8, 'On Trial'

Establishing democracy from 1949

In the decades after the Second World War, West Germany developed into a peaceful, prosperous and mainly stable nation, with a Western-oriented, pro-US foreign policy. Germany became a member of **NATO** and enjoyed substantial economic development (the *Wirtschaftswunder*, or economic miracle) which produced higher living standards. Politics in the era until the mid-1960s was dominated by Chancellor Konrad Adenauer, the first elected leader of post-war West Germany, and his Christian Democratic Union (CDU) party.

The Basic Law

The new Federal Republic of Germany was governed under the terms of a 'Basic Law' which acted as its constitution. The Allies retained a veto on German law and the new state was not free to determine its foreign policy, but the Basic Law saw the restoration of democracy to Germany. Under the Basic Law:

- A *Bundestag* or Federal Parliament, elected by universal suffrage in elections, was to be held every four years. Half of the seats were allocated proportionally, and half on a **first-past-the-post system**. The *Bundestag* debated and passed laws.
- The Chancellor was the head of government and most powerful politician. The Chancellor was appointed by the President, and needed the approval of the *Bundestag*, and was usually the head of the largest party in the *Bundestag*.
- The President had limited, mainly ceremonial powers and was appointed by a **Federal Convention** for a maximum of two five-year terms. The Federal Convention was made up of half *Bundestag* members and half members of local state parliaments.
- The *Bundesrat* was made up of members of local state parliaments and had a veto over legislation passed by the *Bundestag*.
- A Federal Constitutional Court could rule on what was constitutional.
- FRG was a federal system – state Parliaments were elected every four or five years and had considerable powers to enact laws at local level.

The Weimar Constitution and the Basic Law of the FRG

The Basic Law tried to deal with some of the perceived flaws in the Weimar's constitution in order to try to make democracy in Germany stronger and more stable.
- The powers of the President were limited.
- Parties needed to get a minimum of 5 per cent of the vote in order to get any representation in the *Bundestag*, a measure aimed at preventing small extremist parties gaining representation.
- A Chancellor and his government could only be brought down by a vote of no confidence if another party was ready to govern and able to form a government that had the support of more than half of the members of the *Bundestag*.
- Only half of the seats in the *Bundestag* were determined on the basis of proportional representation, in order to try to make it easier to form stable governments.
- The constitutional court upheld basic civil rights and could rule on whether government actions were illegal.
- The Basic Law also emphasised human rights and pledged the government to uphold them.

The CDU and the SPD

The CDU was formed after the Second World War out of the remnants of the Catholic and fairly conservative Centre Party. Catholic conservatism was less tainted by association with the Nazis than other strains of right-wing politics, and Adenauer's CDU built itself into a powerful political force in the new Germany. The new party did not promote itself as a Catholic party, and proved very successful at attracting the votes of right-wing and centrist Protestants. The party also contained Christians who held socialist beliefs, but Adenauer was firmly anti-socialist and a believer in capitalism and a pro-American foreign policy.

The Social Democratic Party (the SPD), which had continued to exist in exile and underground throughout the war, re-established itself in post-war West Germany, initially as a **Marxist** party in favour of the unification of Germany. Their first post-war leader was Kurt Schumacher.

Quick quizzes at www.hoddereducation.co.uk/myrevisionnotes

Spectrum of importance

Below are a sample exam question and a list of general points which could be used to answer the question. Use your own knowledge and the information on the opposite page and elsewhere in this book to reach a judgement about the importance of these general points to the question posed.

Write a number on the spectrum below to indicate their relative importance. Having done this, write a brief justification of your placement, explaining why some of these factors are more important than others. The resulting diagram could form the basic of an essay plan.

> How far were the changes to Germany's constitutional arrangements made in 1949 caused by defeats in war?

1 Defeat in war
2 Breakdown of political systems
3 Impositions by foreign powers

←───→
Least important   Most important

Eliminate irrelevance

Below are a sample exam question and a paragraph written in answer to this question. Read the paragraph and identify parts of the paragraph that are not directly relevant to the question. Draw a line through the information that is irrelevant and justify your deletions in the margin.

> How far do you agree that Constitutional Law in Germany was transformed in the years 1918–49?

Constitutional Law was transformed in Germany between 1918 and 1949 to some extent. The Basic Law constitution introduced in 1949 was in part a return to the Weimar Constitution established in 1919, but it also contained important differences. Weimar is a town in Germany where the constitution was written in 1919. The Basic Law restored democracy to (West) Germany, and like the Weimar system, there were elections to the federal parliament every four years on the basic of universal suffrage. As in the Weimar system, the Chancellor and the government needed the support of the Parliament. However, there were various significant changes in the Basic Law in comparison with the Weimar Constitution which were designed to make democracy in the FRG stronger and more stable than that in Weimar Germany. One difference was that it was not so easy to remove a Chancellor through a vote of no confidence — a new government needed to be ready to be formed and in possession of sufficient support from Parliament. Furthermore, the new system reduced the proportional element in the voting system and made it harder for small extremist parties, such as the Nazis had been, to gain representation. The Nazi Party was founded in 1919 in Munich by Anton Drexler. The President, who was considered to have had too much power in the time of President Hindenburg, had very little power in the FRG, and could only appoint a Chancellor with Bundestag approval. Overall, the new constitution of the FRG was not a transformation in comparison with Weimar's constitution, but it did contain certain major modifications.

Consolidation under Adenauer and Erhard, 1949–66

REVISED

Adenauer in power, 1949–63

Konrad Adenauer, a former Centre Party mayor of Cologne and President of the Prussian State Council who had been imprisoned by the Nazis, was instrumental in the establishment and development of the CDU and became its first leader. In the first West German *Bundestag* elections of August 1949, the CDU emerged as the strongest party and a month later, with the support of the right-wing Free Democrats, 73-year-old Adenauer was chosen by the *Bundestag* to be the first Chancellor of post-War Germany. In power, Adenauer dominated government and pursued certain policies vigorously.

Integration, not denazification

Adenauer denounced the denazification policies and instead launched a policy whereby former Nazis were to be integrated in post-war Germany. Adenauer argued that this was necessary to build a unified and harmonious country. Even when his state secretary, Hans Globke, was revealed to have been involved in drafting anti-Semitic laws in Nazi Germany, Adenauer refused to sack him. He also called upon the Allies to commute the sentences of those convicted of war crimes.

Restitution

Adenauer did, however, believe that Germany needed to make amends to the Jewish people for Nazi crimes against them, and supported the formation of a **Claims Conference** for Jewish victims of Nazism and also the payment of large reparations to Israel, as the representative of the Jewish people. This payment of 3 billion Deutschmarks to Israel was pushed through by Adenauer with SPD support, in the face of opposition from many Germany people and many in the CDU. The **German Restitution Laws** were passed in 1953, although they were limited in their scope.

Western-oriented foreign policy

Adenauer believed that the future of Germany lay with a Western-oriented (that is, US- and French-orientated) foreign policy, and with this in mind, he rejected Stalin's (probably insincere) overtures about possibility creating an independent and **non-aligned** unified German state in 1952. He pushed for Germany's membership of the US-dominated security alliance NATO, which was attained in 1955 in return for various German pledges committing to limiting their future military capabilities. Adenauer was instrumental in creating a degree of unity with France through the creation of the **European Coal and Steel Community**.

The Berlin Wall

Construction of the Berlin Wall was started in August 1961 by the East German government to separate the Communist eastern part of the city from the west. The East German government claimed its construction was to prevent infiltration in East Germany, but in fact its primary purpose was to stop emigration from the east to the west. The Wall came to symbolise divided Germany.

A social market economy

Adenauer and Economics Minister Ludwig Erhard pursued a **mixed economic model**, combining capitalism with social welfare (see page 88). This helped create social harmony, and along with the strong economic growth of the post-1950 era, helped to create legitimacy and stability in the FRG.

Later years

Following his success in assuring the return of the final 10,000 German prisoners of war held by the Soviet Union, Adenauer's CDU won a strong victory in the 1957 election. Later this year he supported the formation of the **European Economic Community (EEC)**, which further strengthened links with France. Adenauer stepped down from power in 1963 after a scandal implicating the government in repressive practices, and died in 1967 at the age of 91.

A new Chancellor: Ludwig Erhard, 1963–66

Ludwig Erhard, who had been a highly successful Economics Minister under Adenauer, and prior to that Director of Economics for the British and American occupied zones, became Chancellor of West Germany in 1963. Erhard unsuccessfully pursued German reunification, and resigned following budgetary difficulties in 1966.

Develop the detail

Below are a sample exam question and a paragraph written in answer to this question. The paragraph contains a limited amount of detail. Annotate the paragraph to add additional detail to the answer.

> How accurate is it to say that between 1949 and 1989 the government of the Federal Republic of Germany was economically strong and politically stable?

In many respects the government of the Federal Republic of Germany was strong and stable. The Chancellors of the FRG were generally in power for fairly long periods of time and they presided over stable governments. This was particularly true during the time that Konrad Adenauer was Chancellor. Adenauer was Chancellor for a long time and did not face any votes of no confidence. Stability was also created by his policy of the social market economy. The government of Ludwig Erhard was not so strong and stable, and it only lasted for three years before he resigned.

Support your judgement

Below are a sample exam question and two basic judgements. Read the exam question and the two judgements. Support the judgement that you agree with most strongly by adding a reason that justifies the judgement.

> How far was Konrad Adenauer responsible for the strength and stability of the FRG's political system between 1949 and 1963?

Overall, Adenauer was responsible for the FRG's strong and stable political system to some degree
_____
_____

Adenauer was responsible for FRG's strong and stable political system to a significant degree
_____
_____

Tip: whichever option you choose you will have to weigh up both sides of the argument. You could use phrases such as 'whereas' or words like 'although' in order to help the process of evaluation.

Economic recovery and the 'economic miracle', 1945–66

In the years after the establishment of the FRG, West Germany enjoyed strong economic growth, low inflation and rising living standards. The transformation from war devastation to a global economic power was labelled an 'economic miracle' – *Wirtschaftswunder*.

The *Wirtschaftswunder*, 1950–60

Jobs	The unemployment rate fell from 11 per cent to only 1.2 per cent.
Economic growth	National income almost doubled from 845 billion Deutschmarks to 1,633 billion.
Industrial development	Industrial development increased by 150 per cent. New industrial developments such as VW at Wolfsburg were developed.
Living standards	Real incomes rose after 1952.

Causes of the *Wirtschaftswunder*

The Deutschmark, 1948

In June 1948 a new currency, the Deutschmark (DM), was introduced into the non-Soviet zones of Germany to replace the Reichsmark (RM). Wage levels in DM were at the same level as for RM, but savings were exchanged at a very low level of 6.5DM to 100RM. Savers were very badly hit, but debts of some 400 billion RM were written off, which gave a much-needed stimulus to the economy.

The end of price controls

On the same day as the introduction of the new currency, Ludwig Erhard, in his role as Director of Economics in the British and American zones, ended price controls. This had the effect of increasing the supply of goods to the market. This reform stimulated the economy and contributed to economic recovery.

Loans for industry and high levels of public and private investment

Banks were given money by authorities to loan to businesses to get industrial investment restarted. Industrial investment increased by 50 per cent following this move. In addition to the loans, greater stability was created by the currency reforms, and after a few years of peace helped to encourage business to feel confident to invest. The Investment Aid Law of 1952 provided subsidies to assist with industrial development.

Local authorities also invested heavily in transport, educational, social and cultural infrastructure at this time. Job creation schemes were developed from 1950.

Tax cuts

Tax cuts helped to stimulate the economy by increasing the money that people had to spend, which in turn increased production of goods. For those on lower incomes, the tax level was reduced to 18 per cent.

The Marshall Plan

The $1.5 billion transferred to Germany from the USA under the **Marshall Plan** helped to rebuild German infrastructure and generate confidence.

The social market economy

The mixed economic model proved highly successful in creating economic growth and maintaining stability in West Germany. The country combined capitalist free enterprise with governmental oversight to prevent unfair practices, and the ownership by the state of parts of the economy, such as the railways, and state provision of welfare services. Furthermore, the model of worker involvement in commercial enterprises, often established by British managers in occupied Germany in plants such as VW after the war, was extended. Workers' representatives sat on the boards of German companies and had a right to be consulted about major decisions. This helped maintain harmony between workers and management, which assisted with economic development.

Other factors behind the *Wirtschaftswunder*

Other factors included the development of a trade surplus, as German manufactured goods proved popular round the world. The surpluses could be invested in further development. Furthermore, Germany had an educated workforce, many raw materials and good sea ports for exporting goods. In addition, the pursuit of cooperation and integration with other European states such as France in the EEC (see page 94) helped with economic stability and development and promoted lower tariffs, which helped to stimulate international trade.

Establish criteria

Below is a sample exam question which requires you to make a judgement. The key term in the question has been underlined. Defining the meaning of the key term can help you establish criteria that you can use to make a judgement.

Read the question, define the key term and then set out two or three criteria based on the key term, which you can use to reach and justify a judgement.

> How accurate is it to say that the government's economic policies <u>were effective</u> in Germany and the FRG between 1933 and 1966?

Definition:

Criteria:

Reach a judgement

Having defined the key term and established a series of criteria, you should now make a judgement. Consider how far the government's economic policies were effective in Germany and the FRG between 1933 and 1966 according to each criterion. Summarise your judgements below.

Criterion 1:

Criterion 2:

Criterion 3:

Criterion 4:

The nature of support for democracy in the FRG, 1949–66

REVISED

The democratic regime was generally widely supported during the period 1949–66 and moderate, centrist politics were popular.

Support for the system

After the devastating defeat that fascism had produced, the majority of people in the FRG supported the new democratic regime. The successes it had in economic policy and the support it had from powerful countries such as the USA helped to bolster support for the regime. Support for the system is indicated in the high turnouts in elections (generally 80–90 per cent) in the FRG and in the lack of support that extremists received.

Party political support

The Christian Democrats (CDU/CSU)

The CDU and its allied sister party, the Christian Social Union of Bavaria (CSU), dominated politics in Germany in the years after the establishment of the FRG. As 50 per cent of West Germany was Catholic, the Catholic roots of the CDU/CSU had widespread appeal and its conservative stance appealed to many Protestants, too. The success that the CDU-led governments under Adenauer had with economic policy and living standards in the early years of the FRG helped boost support for the CDU/CSU. The party moved politically to the centre and supported the creation of a welfare state and a social market economy. These policies, and its pro-Western foreign policy, were popular. The incorporation of workers' representatives in management structures in industry also helped to create stability and, in turn, support for the CDU/CSU. Support for the CDU in elections grew from 31 per cent in 1949 to 50.2 per cent by 1957.

The Social Democrats (SPD)

The Social Democrats had survived underground since the Nazi era, and might have been expected to resume their position as the most popular party, as they had been in Germany since 1912. The party did pick up large amounts of support from workers, but the successes of the Christian Democrats and the radicalism of the SPD reduced their appeal and meant that they struggled to gain enough votes to form a government, and in 1959 the SPD gained 32 per cent of the vote. In response to this, in 1959, the SPD dropped their anti-clerical policies, which were not very popular in with many Germans, and moved away from Marxist politics to adopt a moderate centre-left position. This left the party in a good position to profit from growing disillusionment with the CDU/CSU from the mid-1960s, but it also caused disillusionment with the SPD, and fuelled the more radical '**new left**' movements (see page 96).

Establish criteria

Below is a sample exam question which requires you to make a judgement. The key term in the question has been underlined. Defining the meaning of the key term can help you establish criteria that you can use to make a judgement.

Read the question, define the key term and then set out two or three criteria based on the key term, which you can use to reach and justify a judgement.

How far were politics in West Germany <u>characterised by consensus</u> in the years 1949–74?

Definition:

_____

_____

Criteria:

_____

_____

_____

Turning assertion into argument

Below are a sample exam question and a series of assertions. Read the exam question and then add a justification to each of the assertions to turn it into an argument.

How far were politics in West Germany characterised by consensus in the years 1949–74?

Overall, Adenauer was responsible for the FRG's strong and stable political system to some degree

_____

_____

Successes in economic policy and rising living standards helped to boost the consensus about the democratic political system in West Germany in that

_____

_____

After the SPD moved to the centre in 1959, there was a degree of consensus between the two main parties in that

_____

_____

Maintaining political stability under Brandt, Schmidt and Kohl, 1966–89

REVISED

From the mid-1960s, the FRG faced increasing strains as relations deteriorated with East Germany following the construction of the Berlin Wall in 1961, and the economy did not grow as strongly. Ludwig Erhard was replaced as Chancellor and leader of the Christian Democrats by Kurt Kiesinger, who entered into a 'Grand Coalition' with the SPD. SPD leader **Willy Brandt** became deputy Chancellor and Foreign Minister. Kiesinger's government fell in the face of rising criticism of his government's authoritarian tendencies (see page 98) and Kiesinger's status as an ex-member of the Nazi party.

Willy Brandt in power, 1969–74

The SPD had been growing in popularity partly because of the support they received from the young. Willy Brandt, who had been involved in active underground resistance to the Nazis during the war, represented a more comprehensive break with Germany's Nazi past, and he had also won widespread acclaim for his principled opposition to the construction of the Berlin Wall. There were great expectations for Brandt's government but, as the economy continued to struggle and inflation developed in the 1970s, many were disappointed. Brandt's governments also faced challenges from political extremists (see page 96). Brandt did succeed, through his *Ostpolitik* ('East Politics'), in normalising relations with East Germany. As part of *Ostpolitik*:

- Brandt visited East Germany and the two Germanies recognised each other as independent states in 1973.
- *Ostpolitik* saw Brandt improve relations with communist Eastern Europe more generally, something perhaps best represented by his visit to Poland in 1970, during which he signed an agreement recognising Poland's post-war borders.
- Also on this visit, in a gesture symbolising German remorse for the war and the Holocaust, Brandt dropped to his knees at the **Warsaw Ghetto** memorial.
- Despite domestic ambivalence about these measures, their success ensured Brandt obtained a victory in the 1972 elections.

He resigned in 1974 when a close advisor was found to be an East German spy.

Helmut Schmidt in power, 1974–82

Helmut Schmidt, Brandt's Economics Minister, took over as Chancellor. Schmidt continued with *Ostpolitik* and formed a coalition with the Free Democratic Party (FDP) after 1974. Tensions developed between the two parties, however, and Schmidt faced difficulties in dealing with inflation and the rise of the Green movement (see page 96). He lost a vote of no confidence in the Bundestag in October 1982 and resigned.

FRG governments, 1966–89

Dates	Governing party / coalition	Chancellor
1966–69	Grand Coalition – Christian Democrats / SPD	Kurt Kiesinger
1969–76	SPD / Free Democrats	Willy Brandt
1976–83	SPD / Free Democrats	Helmut Schmidt
1983–90	Christian Democrats / Free Democrats	Helmut Kohl

Helmut Kohl in power, 1982–90

Schmidt was replaced by Christian Democrat **Helmut Kohl**. Kohl continued with *Ostpolitik* and worked to develop European integration with the EEC. He worked with President Reagan of the USA and General Secretary Mikhail Gorbachev of the Soviet Union to bring an end to the Cold War.

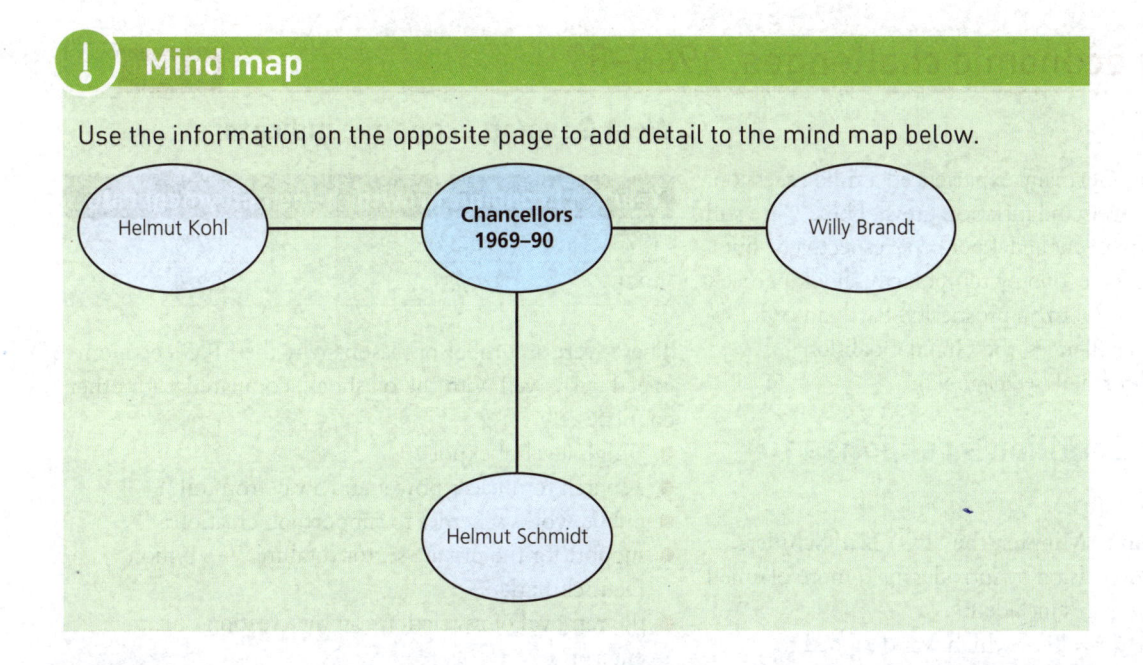

⚠ Mind map

Use the information on the opposite page to add detail to the mind map below.

- Helmut Kohl
- **Chancellors 1969–90**
- Willy Brandt
- Helmut Schmidt

ⓘ Recommended reading

Below is a list of suggested further reading on this topic.
- Viola Herms Drath, *Willy Brandt – Prisoner of his Past* (reissued, 2005)
- Stephen Padgett (ed.), *Adenauer to Kohl – The Development of the German Chancellorship* (1994)
- Alexander von Plato, translated by Edith Burley, *The End of the Cold War? Bush, Kohl, Gorbachev, and the Reunification of Germany* (2015)

4 Democratic government in West Germany, 1945–89

Surviving economic challenges, 1966–89

Recession

In the mid-1960s, Germany experienced a mild recession. Unemployment levels and inflation grew. These were still fairly low, at 3.8 per cent and 4 per cent respectively, but the downturn in the economy temporarily shook people's confidence in West German prosperity. Partly in order to respond to these challenges, the Grand Coalition government was formed (see page 92).

The Grand Coalition's response to recession

The new Economics Minister, the SPD's Karl Schiller, responded to the recession by introducing a more planned economy. His measures included:

- A Stabilisation Law 1967, which was designed to improve cooperation between federal government, employers and employees in economically difficult times (a policy known as 'concerted action'). The law created the potential for central government powers to increase in order to alter taxes and raise loans to stimulate production.
- Greater central government powers to direct economic policies in the regions of Germany.
- Reducing public spending and raising taxes: VAT went up from 10 to 12 per cent.

These measures proved successful, as unemployment and inflation reduced and Germany's strong economic growth resumed.

Revaluation

From the late 1960s, strong demand for the Deutschmark and a high level of exports meant that there was pressure to revalue the currency to make its value higher in relation to other currencies. The Grand Coalition could not agree on a policy for this, and it collapsed as a result. Willy Brandt's new government proceeded with raising the value of the currency by more than 9 per cent. Despite the fact that this move increased the cost of German exports to foreign consumers, German goods had a reputation for quality and continued to be popular abroad.

The 1973 Oil Shock

Post-war European economic growth had relied upon cheap imports of oil. In October 1973, however, the Organization of Petroleum Exporting Countries (OPEC) announced that its members would increase the price of oil by 70 per cent while also reducing output by 5 per cent. This oil price 'shock' had the effect of significantly increasing the cost of production in oil-importing countries, such as West Germany. The FRG's economy was hit by the oil shock, and unemployment rose, but overall the West German economy coped quite well with the crisis.

West German economic indicators

Year	Economic growth	Unemployment rate
1973	5.3%	1.2%
1975	0.4%	4.7%

There were a number of reasons why the FRG's economy coped fairly well with the oil shock, compared with other countries:

- a high level of exports
- a switch to nuclear power and away from oil
- public works schemes to support job creation
- support for the private sector totalling 7–8 billion Deutschmarks
- the removal of restrictions on the creation of larger enterprises
- the extension of the role of the EEC benefitted Germany.

The EEC

The European Economic Community was formed by the **Treaty of Rome** in 1957. The Community built on the success of the European Coal and Steel Community (see page 86). The founder members were West Germany, France, Italy, the Netherlands, Belgium and Luxembourg. Its aim was to promote European harmony and prosperity through creating a common market and a customs union. In 1973, the United Kingdom, Ireland and Denmark had also joined the EEC. In 1978, under Helmut Schmidt's leadership, a European Monetary System (EMS) was created in order to harmonise the currencies of Europe and try to prevent inflation. The Deutschmark became the key currency in the setting of exchange rates for currencies in the EMS.

Delete as applicable

Below are a sample exam question and a paragraph written in answer to this question. Read the paragraph and decide which of the possible options (in bold) is most appropriate. Delete the least appropriate options and complete the paragraph by justifying your selection.

> How accurate is it to say that the governments of the FRG dealt with economic challenges effectively between 1966 and 1989?

It is accurate to say that the FRG dealt with the oil shock of 1973 effectively between 1966 and 1989 to a **limited/fair/considerable** extent. This was partly because of the strengths of the German economy, such as the high quality of the goods that it produced for export, but was also because of concerted government action. The West German government took steps to reduce the country's dependency on oil by, for example, investing in nuclear fuel. They also took measures to support German industry at this challenging time, and provided over 7 billion Deutschmarks for this purpose. Furthermore, the government tried to reduce the effect that the oil shock might have on unemployment by investing in public works schemes. Overall, while unemployment did rise and economic growth fell substantially, the FRG still coped better than most other countries with the oil crisis, and in this sense, dealt with this particular economic challenge **very/somewhat/not very** effectively.

_____

_____

Simple essay style

Below is a sample exam question. Use your own knowledge and the information on the opposite page to produce a plan for this question. Choose four general points and provide two or three pieces of specific information to support each general point.

Once you have planned your essay, write the introduction and conclusion for the essay. The introduction should list the points to be discussed in the essay. The conclusion should summarise the key points and justify which point was the most important.

> How accurate is it to say that the governments of the FRG managed economic challenges effectively between 1966 and 1989?

Political dissent and active challenge, 1949–89

In the first few years after the end of the Second World War, active opposition to the new state was rare. The exhaustion caused by war and total defeat, along with the rising levels of prosperity, might account for this. From the 1960s, however, some people, particularly the young, became involved in 'new left' opposition movements. The participants were often frustrated by the limits of German democracy and the country's failure to confront its Nazi past. A generational conflict developed between the middle-aged and old, who did not want to talk about the past, and the young, post-war generation. Mass protests and sit-ins characterised the actions of the student movement, while extremist anti-capitalists the Red Army Faction (RAF) launched a sustained campaign of terrorism.

The student movement

Underfunding, teacher shortages and lack of student representation at German universities caused tensions among German students from the mid-1960s. The Free University in West Berlin became a particular site of student discontent. The student movement came increasingly under the influence of the radical leftist Socialist German Students' Union (SDS). Under the leadership of Rudi Dutschke, the SDS campaigned on a wide range of issues, including against the Vietnam War, against **nuclear proliferation** and to try to prevent former Nazis retaining positions of power in the FRG. In response to students' protests in 1965 and 1966, the government increased expenditure on higher education.

In the late 1960s, the student movement continued to engage in protest and in new forms of living, such as communes. In 1968, during the global upsurge of protest that occurred during that year, Rudi Dutschke was shot by a neo-Nazi, an event that provoked massive protests. The student movement lacked support from most of wider society and its influence began to wane in the late 1960s. Dutschke advocated peaceful change in society, but some of those involved began to endorse more radical methods from this time.

Radical politics and the Red Army Faction (RAF)

The radical leftist group the Red Army Faction (which received financial backing from the East German state) sought an end to consumerist capitalist society and were also opposed to the Vietnam War. The RAF believed that radical action was the only way to achieve change in society. The group was also known as the Baader-Meinhof gang after two of its members, Ulrike Meinhof and Andreas Baader, were involved in radical action such as the bombing of a department store in Frankfurt in 1968. In the 1970s the group turned to assassination and kidnapping. In total, 28 people were murdered by the RAF and many others were injured. RAF bombings and murders continued into the 1980s, but the extremism of the group had alienated many voters that might otherwise have supported some of their political positions. The group finally announced its dissolution in 1998.

The RAF and the German Autumn

In 1977, the Red Army Faction's activities reached their peak during the events known as the *Deutscher Herbst* (German Autumn):

- The RAF targeted prominent and powerful figures and in April 1977 assassinated the West German Attorney General, Siegfried Buback.
- In July, the group killed the head of the Dresdner Bank, Jürgen Ponto.
- The most dramatic events occurred in autumn 1977. On 5 September, the RAF kidnapped Hans Martin Schleyer, President of the German Employers' Association and a former member of the SS, in an ambush that killed four others. The RAF forced Schleyer to appeal to the government for the release of RAF members held in jail. Three of these, including Baader, were found dead in their cells on 18 October, and the RAF murdered Schleyer in response and hijacked a plane, the *Landshut*.

Neo-Nazism

A number of small neo-Nazi groups continued to exist in the FRG, including the Socialist Reich Party (see page 98). These groups unified into the National Democratic Party (NDP) in 1964. This party never achieved the 5 per cent of the vote required to attain representation in the *Bundestag*, however – although on occasion, it did achieve more success at local level.

The Green Party

From the 1980s, the establishment and development of the Green Party provided a democratic and peaceful outlet for those who politically opposed the mainstream politics of the Christian Democrats and the SPD. Feminists also often became involved in the Green Party. The existence of the Green Party may have been one reason why there was less extremist activity in Germany during the 1980s.

Mind map

Use the information on the opposite page to add detail to the mind map below.

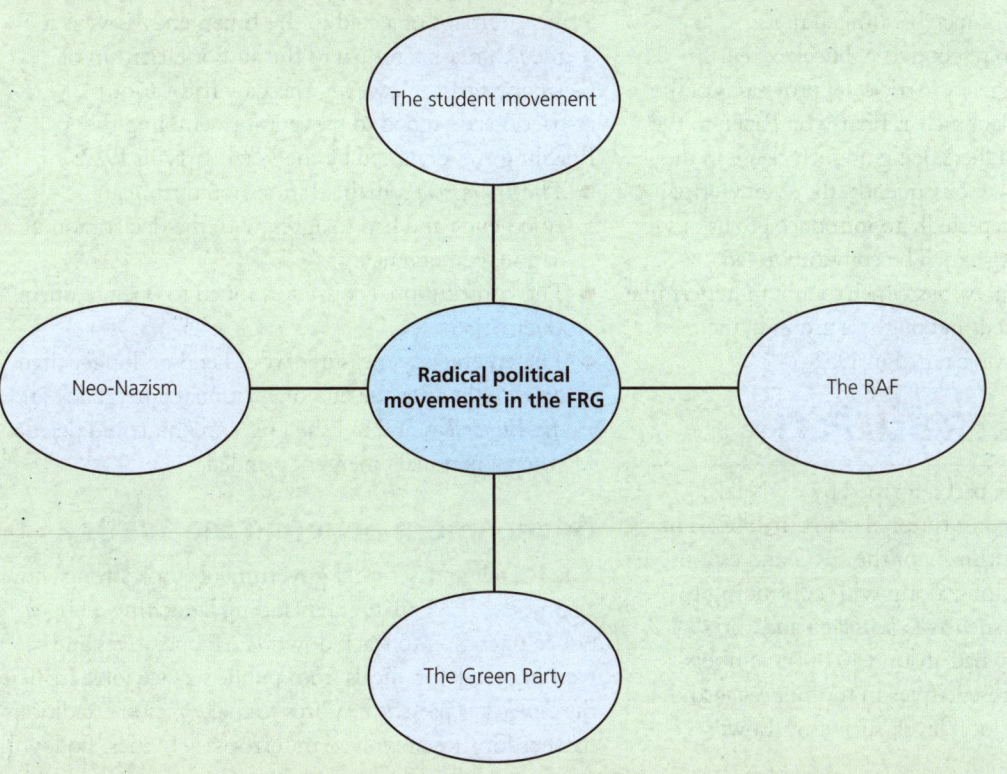

- The student movement
- Neo-Nazism
- **Radical political movements in the FRG**
- The RAF
- The Green Party

Identify key terms

Below is a sample question which includes a key word or term. Key terms are important because their meaning can be helpful in structuring your answer, developing an argument and establishing criteria that will help form the basis of a judgement.

How accurate is it to say that there was strong popular support for the political system of the FRG between 1949 and 1989?

- First, identify the key term. This will be a word or phrase that is important to the meaning of the question. Underline the word or phrase.
- Second, define the key phrase. Your definition should set out the key features of the phrase that you are defining.
- Third, make an essay plan that reflects your definition.
- Finally, write a sentence answering the question that refers back to the definition.

Now repeat the task using the question below, and consider how the change in key terms affects the argument, structure and final judgement of your essay.

How accurate is it to say that there was little effective opposition to the political system of the FRG between 1949 and 1989?

The constitutional and legal response to political extremism, 1949–89

The FRG was initially somewhat limited in its constitutional ability to respond to political extremism. The subversion of the emergency 'Article 48' provisions of the constitution by politicians such as Franz von Papen in the Weimar era resulted in there being no such clause in the new FRG constitution. Consequently, the West German authorities attempted repeatedly to introduce provisions for them to act in an emergency. The constitution did, however, allow political parties which sought to undermine democracy to be banned, and on these grounds, the Socialist Reich Party was banned in 1952.

The Socialist Reich Party

This essentially Nazi party, formed by ex-Nazis, was banned by the constitutional court in 1952. The party denied the legitimacy of the FRG and espoused vaguely socialist notions, along with continuing to promote Nazi ideas such as *Lebensraum* and anti-Semitism. The party had around 10,000 members, and gained two representatives in the *Bundestag* and a number of seats at local level, such as in Lower Saxony in 1951.

Emergency powers

In 1958, 1960 and 1963 attempts were made to introduce legislation which would provide for the extension of the powers of the government in the event of a national emergency. These all failed, as the SPD did not support this move. However, after 1965, as part of the Grand Coalition, the SPD changed its stance. In May 1968, following a number of years of student protests, the emergency legislation finally became law and was written into the constitution. The emergency powers gave the government the power to suspend civil liberties and intercept mail, tap phones and search homes.

Some Germans objected to the Emergency Law as it seemed to mark a return to the authoritarianism of Germany's past. However, the Law had various restrictions designed to prevent it resembling the Enabling Act designed by the Nazi Party in 1933:
- The *Bundestag* remained in session during an emergency and had to agree with the declaration of a national emergency.
- The constitutional court continued to operate during an emergency.
- The emergency measures would end no longer than six months after the end of a national emergency and the *Bundestag*, and not the government, could decide when a national emergency ended.

Government action in the 1970s

The Brandt and Schmidt governments took strong action against the RAF in 1972, including launching a huge police operation to track down RAF operatives and banning far-left radicals from public service jobs. In 1973, the *Bundestag* passed measures to make prison conditions harsher for those involved in terrorist activities. Following the events of the 'German Autumn' (see page 96), measures were adopted which restricted the rights of RAF members in prison to communicate with each other or their lawyers, preventing the RAF from publically disseminating their ideas. In total, 6,000 people were placed under police surveillance.

Government action in the 1980s

As the threat from the RAF declined, the government in the 1980s focused upon rooting out neo-Nazi groups, and a number of these were banned.

Turning assertion into argument

Below are a sample essay question and three assertions. Read the exam question, then add a justification to each assertion to turn it into an argument.

How significant were the challenges made to West German democracy in the years 1949–89?

Radical political parties were only a limited threat to democracy because
_____

Extremist groups in West Germany posed a real challenge to the democratic system because
_____

The actions which the government took against political extremism were successful because
_____

Identify an argument

Below are a series of definitions, a sample exam question and two sample conclusions. One of the conclusions achieves a higher mark because it contains an argument. The other achieves a lower mark because it contains only description and assertion. Identify which is which. The mark scheme on page 113 will help you.

- **Description:** a detailed account.
- **Assertion:** a statement of fact or an opinion which is not supported by a reason.
- **Reason:** a statement which explains or justifies something.
- **Argument:** an assertion justified with a reason.

To what extent was there continuity in the treatment of opponents of the political systems in Germany and West Germany between 1933 and 1989?

Overall, there was continuity in the treatment of opponents to the political system in the Nazi era and in West Germany to some extent. A degree of continuity can be found in some of the authoritarian aspects of policies of the FRG, such as in the surveillance and phone tapping that occurred in the 1970s. Opponents were also imprisoned in harsh conditions in both systems. However, the treatment of opponents of the system in Nazi Germany was far more repressive. People were executed or held without trial. Furthermore, people might be persecuted for very minor acts of opposition – in contrast, those imprisoned in the FRG tended to have committed far more serious crimes. In conclusion, the continuity between the two systems in this area was only fairly limited.

In conclusion, opponents of the political systems were imprisoned during both the Nazi era and in the FRG. The members of the Red Army faction were an example of this, although they had committed crimes such as bombing and kidnapping. There was also surveillance and phone tapping. In the Nazi era, there was also a system of concentration camps and people could be locked up for any reason or none. Some opponents of the regime were executed, such as members of the White Rose. This was very repressive. Even minor acts of opposition might be enough to result in persecution. The FRG was, however, essentially a democracy.

Changing living standards, 1945–89

Living standards increased dramatically from the time of the end of the Second World War until the 1980s. The FRG became a prosperous consumer society with one the highest standards of living in the world.

Consumer spending

A sign of prosperity was that between 1950 and 1965, the level of car ownership increased six-fold to approximately 12 million cars. By the 1980s, 95 per cent of West Germans owned items such as washing machines and televisions, and went on two holidays a year.

The cost of living

In West Germany there was a plentiful supply of consumer goods and low inflation, which meant that it was a very affordable place to live. By 1989, the cost of living in Britain was some 25 per cent higher than that in the FRG. High levels of productivity growth (that is, the economic output produced by each worker) between 1950 and the mid-1970s helped to drive improved living standards. The cost of basic foodstuffs also fell, which helped support rising living standards. The cost of living did not always continually improve, particularly in the 1970s, when inflation increased to 6 per cent. However, fairly harmonious relations between German workers and their employers meant that while trade unions generally helped to maintain living standards as prices increased (by asking for higher wages for their members), demands for wage rises were generally moderate. This also helped restrict inflation. From the mid-1980s, the cost of living started to fall again, and once again living standards rose.

Housing

In the early years of the FRG, there was a housing shortage which saw many families share homes – 4 million houses had been destroyed by Allied bombing during the war. As more houses were constructed over the years, this practice ended and the amount of living space for each family increased. The average amount of space each person had in their dwelling rose from 19 square metres in 1950 to 30 square metres in 1980. The quality of housing also improved gradually, with, for example, a reduction in the number of homes with an outside toilet.

Education policies in the FRG

In the immediate post-war period, the occupying authorities rushed to try to denazify the German education system. New curricula and textbooks were quickly brought out, and German teachers were sent on re-education programmes. The British and the French authorities sent some British and French teachers to teach in Germany, while the US authorities invested heavily in resources for German schools and established a training programme for German teachers in the USA.

Mind map

Use the information on the opposite page and elsewhere in this book to add detail to the mind map below.

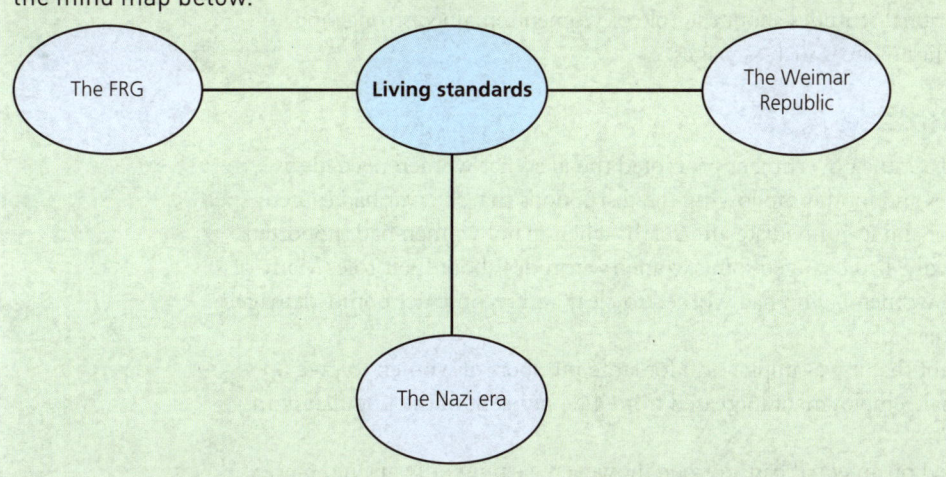

- The FRG — **Living standards** — The Weimar Republic
- The Nazi era

Develop the detail

Below is a sample exam question and a paragraph written in answer to this question. The paragraph contains a limited amount of detail. Annotate the paragraph to add additional detail to the answer.

> How accurate is it to say that living standards in Germany and the FRG rose continuously between 1933 and 1989?

In the FRG, there were many improvements in living standards, and living standards did generally rise continually, with the exception perhaps of a small blip in the 1970s. The standard of living rose because people had more disposable income. West Germany became a consumerist society and people had access to modern consumer goods. Furthermore, people's standard of living rose because the quality of housing, so damaged during the Second World War, rose.

The role and status of women in the FRG

The constitution of the FRG proclaimed that men and women were equal, so it might be expected that the role and status of women in the FRG would be significantly different to that in the Nazi era. However, traditional attitudes about the role of women remained strong, and women did not achieve equality in areas such as wages.

Women in the workplace

- In the early years of the FRG, the government promoted the idea that women needed to return to their role as wives and mothers following the disruptions that the war had caused.
- The experience of wartime and its immediate aftermath, when many women had supported their families single-handedly, had changed some women's attitudes about their role. Many of the *Trümmerfrauen* ('rubble women'), who had worked to clear and reconstruct bomb-damaged areas, refused to give up their jobs.
- Labour shortages also meant that it was impractical for large numbers of women to give up their jobs. The rate of female employment increased from 44.4 per cent of the population in 1950 to 50 per cent in 1970.
- Women were not employed on an equal basis to men, however, earning only around 65–78 per cent of the rate of men for similar occupations.
- Women also tended to be employed predominantly in a restricted range of occupations, such as caring and nursing.
- In areas such as politics, women did not tend to have positions of power and still only occupied around 15 per cent of representatives in the *Bundestag* by the late 1980s, and there were only small numbers of women in managerial roles in most parts of the economy.

Most Germans, including many women, continued to feel that a woman's role was as homemaker and carer for her children, and the attitude that women with small children should not work at all remained widespread.

Feminism, divorce and abortion law and the Greens

Despite the persistence of inequality and traditional views about the proper role of women, changes did occur to the role and status of women. From the 1960s onwards, some German women began to embrace feminist ideas that challenged inequality and the idea that women should be restricted to certain roles in society.

Partly as a result of the work of this movement, divorce law was changed in 1977 to allow for no-fault divorce and also the provision of financial support to a dependent spouse who had given up work to support a family.

Abortion law was also altered in 1976 to allow for abortion in the first 12 weeks of pregnancy in certain circumstances. Feminists felt that the law was too restrictive, but the law was not changed during the existence of the FRG.

In the political arena, the success of the Green Party saw more women became involved in politics.

Simple essay style

Below is a sample exam question. Use your own knowledge and the information on the opposite page and elsewhere in this book to produce a plan for this question. Choose four general points and provide two or three pieces of specific information to support each point.

Once you have planned your essay, write the introduction and conclusion for the essay. The introduction should list the points to be discussed in the essay. The conclusion should summarise the key points and justify which point was the most important.

> How accurate is it to say that women's roles as mothers and homemakers remained unchanged in Germany and West Germany in the years 1918–89?

Develop the detail

Below are a sample exam question and a paragraph written in answer to this question. The paragraph contains a limited amount of detail. Annotate the paragraph to add additional detail to the answer.

> How far did the role of women in Germany and West Germany change in the years 1918–89?

To some extent, the role of women in West Germany changed compared to the Nazi era. More women worked, and some women became actively involved in politics. However, traditional attitudes about the role of women remained strong and, particularly in the early years of the FRG, women were encouraged to return to the home, after many of them had become involved in paid work during the Second World War. The idea that women with children should not work was a widely held belief. Furthermore, even though many women worked, they did not earn as much as men in the same roles. It was only in the 1970s that more change occurred to the role of women, as some women embraced feminism, and divorce and abortion law became more liberal. In the 1980s, the Green movement saw more women becoming actively involved in politics. There were, then, some changes to the role of women in the era of the FRG compared with the Nazi era and Weimar eras, but the traditional idea of women as homemakers with children remained in place.

The status of, and attitudes towards, ethnic minorities in the FRG

REVISED

In the FRG, minorities still faced discrimination and the state did not treat foreign 'guest workers', who were often Turkish, as equal citizens.

Guest workers in the 1950s

As West Germany's economy grew in the 1950s, the country needed an increased labour supply. The government looked to foreign workers to fill the gap, but did not want these people to emigrate permanently to FRG with their families. In the mid-1950s, the West German government signed an agreement with Italy that would see 100,000 Italian workers come to Germany. Workers from Yugoslavia were also encouraged to come. The 'guest workers' were given temporary contracts, and were not entitled to citizenship, as entitlement to German citizenship was based upon 'German heritage', rather than residency or even birth.

Turkish guest workers in the 1960s

In 1961, the West German government signed an agreement with the Turkish government to bring hundreds of thousands of Turkish workers to Germany as 'guest workers'. Most worked in Germany's major industrial centres. By the end of 1964, 1 million guest workers had come to Germany. Many did not return home, but stayed on and continually renewed their work permits. More and more guest worker families were based in Germany, and the government increasingly provided services such as basic accommodation to these families, in recognition of their crucial role in the economy.

Problems and discrimination in the 1970s

The increasing permanence of guest worker families and the economic downturn in the 1970s provoked some prejudiced and discriminatory attitudes in the FRG. As in other European countries, there was anti-immigration sentiment in West Germany. In late 1979 and 1980, there were even attacks on Jewish memorials and guest worker accommodation.

The state also did not treat the children of guest workers as German citizens, even when they were born and fully educated in Germany, and some were deported when they turned 18. Furthermore, the state started to incentivise guest workers to return home during the economic problems of the 1970s, a policy which many guest workers viewed with resentment.

More and more Turkish families lived in German neighbourhoods and not in the separated guest worker accommodation, however, and became a permanent part of German society.

The 1980s

In the 1980s there were increasing restrictions on immigration to Germany, but also increased recognition of the right of guest workers and their families to settle in Germany.

Delete as applicable

Below are a sample exam question and a paragraph written in answer to this question. Read the paragraph and decide which of the possible options (in bold) is the most appropriate. Delete the least appropriate options and complete the paragraph by justifying your selection.

How far were there continuities in the treatment of ethnic minorities and foreign workers in Germany and West Germany in the years 1933–89?

There were continuities in the treatment of ethnic minorities and foreign workers between the Nazi era and the FRG to a **limited/moderate/significant** extent. In the FRG, citizenship was not based upon residency or even birth, but upon the notion of being ethnically German. This has some parallels with the exclusion of Jews from German citizenship, as the idea was still based on spurious ideas of what it meant to be 'German'. However, those excluded from citizenship in Nazi Germany had no rights and faced persecution. In the FRG, the human rights of 'guest workers' were protected, and their children were educated in German schools. Similarly to the Nazi era, foreign workers in the FRG were often housed separately from the rest of society. Unlike in Nazi Germany, however, many families did move eventually to ordinary neighbourhoods and were not held in labour camps. There were, then, **a few/some/many** continuities in the treatment of ethnic minorities and foreign workers in Germany and West Germany between 1933 and 1989.

_____

_____

Turning assertion into argument

Below are a sample exam question and a series of assertions. Read the exam question and then add a justification to each of the assertions to turn it into an argument.

How far did the position of ethnic minorities and foreign workers in Germany and West Germany transform in the years 1932–89?

The Nazi government transformed the position of Jews and Roma minorities in Germany in the 1930s in that
_____

The Nazi government attempted to destroy Jewish and Roma minorities in Germany during the Second World War, through policies which
_____

In the FRG, the treatment of ethnic minorities and foreign workers by the state improved, as
_____

However, unequal status, discrimination and racism remained in the FRG, as
_____

Edexcel AS/A-level History Germany and West Germany 1918–89

Exam focus

REVISED

Below is an exam-style question and a sample question. Read it and the comments around it.

How accurate is it to say that that the government of Germany and West Germany was transformed between the years 1930–63?

> The government of Germany was transformed to a significant extent between 1930 and 1963. However, the democratic government that was re-established in West Germany in 1949 was to some extent a restoration of the political system that had been functioning reasonably effectively at the start of 1930, and in this sense, the government of Germany was temporarily transformed during the Nazi era and immediate post-war years, but ultimately went back to its pre-Nazi state, at least to a degree.
>
> In many respects, the government of Germany was transformed between 1930 and 1963. At the start of 1930, Germany had a coalition government and a powerful head of state in the shape of President Hindenburg. Governments in the Weimar era had often proved themselves to be weak and short-lived, and the Grand Coalition, which had been formed in 1928, collapsed in 1930 over disagreements about economic policy. Hindenburg refused to support his Chancellor, Müller, in these disputes. In contrast, by 1963, West Germany had a much more stable government: Konrad Adenauer had at this point been Chancellor of a Christian Democratic government since 1949. In the West German political system, the President was much weaker and did not have so much power to undermine or replace Chancellors. Chancellors and their governments could also only be removed by the *Bundestag* if another viable government was ready to be formed. Furthermore, the West German political system was only partially proportional and less characterised by political fragmentation, and so it was easier than in the Weimar era to form stable governments.
>
> In some ways, however, the situation in 1963, in comparison with that in 1930, did not represent a transformation. Both systems of government involved multi-party democracy, universal suffrage, general elections every four years, an elected parliament which agreed to laws, an elected President and a federal system with an assembly that represented the regions. The real transformation of government of Germany occurred during the Nazi era, and this was only a temporary transformation.
>
> In the Nazi era 1933–45, democracy in Germany was ended and dictatorship established. The Chancellor, Adolf Hitler, was given dictatorial powers to bypass the *Reichstag* in the Enabling Act of March 1933. In 1934, the office of President was merged with that of Chancellor and Hitler gained even more power. Parliamentary elections were not held after 1933, and even the plebiscites that did occur were not free or fair. Other political parties were banned, trade unions were taken over by the Nazi Party and there was no freedom of the press or freedom of expression. After the Reichstag Fire Decree of February 1933, people could be arrested and held for any reason, or none. Furthermore, normal governmental decision-making procedures did not generally occur during the Nazi era, and there was no longer the rule of law. Policies were determined upon and implemented in a somewhat chaotic situation, and became more and more extreme.

A clear, but balanced answer to the question.

Supporting detail.

All of this contrasted with the situation in both 1930 in Germany and in 1963, when Germany and West Germany were functioning democracies largely governed by the rule or law, and with political and civil rights guaranteed and decision-making processes that involved the cabinet and the *Bundestag*. The transformation that occurred in the government of Germany was thus largely during the Nazi era, when a dictatorship characterised by repressive policies and ever-growing extremism was established.

German government was transformed once again in the immediate post-war era, after Germany had lost the war and had to submit to foreign occupation. At this time, while some German politicians (such as Ludwig Erhard as Director of Economics) had some power, decisions were often taken by the occupying forces, and could be vetoed by them. The country was also separated in four zones of occupation and governed for a time in this way. Ultimately, two countries emerged – capitalist and democratic West Germany, and communist East Germany. This separation, which remained in 1963, represented another transformation in the government of Germany.

Overall, the government of Germany was transformed to some extent between the years 1930 and 1963. Firstly, it was temporarily transformed during the undemocratic and repressive Nazi era, when free elections, multiple-party democracy, the parliament and the rule of law were ended. Then a further transformation occurred as Germany was occupied and divided. However, in West Germany after 1949, a political system was established which in many ways resembled that of the Weimar era, and so in this sense, government of Germany was not transformed between 1930 and 1963. The situation in 1963 was quite different, however, as a much more stable government emerged in West Germany, compared with the Weimar era.

> The later time period is addressed.

This is a high-level response as it addresses the question directly and provides a clear but balanced answer to the question. It is also supported by a range of specific detail.

> **What makes a good answer?**
>
> You have now considered three high-level essays. Use these essays to make a bullet-point list of the characteristics of a top-level essay. Use this list when planning and writing your own practice exam essays.

AS-level questions

Was political stability in Germany the main consequence of the 'economic miracle' between the years 1949 and 1963? Explain your answer.

How far do you agree that there was a high degree of support for the political system in Germany in the years 1963–89?

To what extent were ethnic minorities in Germany treated as equal citizens in the years 1961–89?

Glossary

Aktion T4 Nazi programme to kill mentally and physically ill and disabled people, which officially ran from 1939–41, but which continued secretly afterwards. It resulted in the murder of more than 200,000 people. The programme was sometimes referred to as euthanasia, when it was in fact murder.

Anschluss Union of Germany and Austria.

Appeasement Policy of making concessions to an aggressor to try to avoid a war.

Aryanisation Nazi policy, from 1938, of seizing Jewish property and giving it to non-Jewish 'Aryans'.

Asocials Those excluded from the Nazi national community because they exhibited behaviour not in keeping with Nazi ideology, such as alcoholism, homosexuality or vagrancy.

Autarkic An economy that is self-sufficient.

Bauhaus Modern school of design founded in Germany in 1919.

Bergen-Belsen Nazi concentration camp liberated by the British in April 1945, who found around 13,000 unburied corpses on the site and around 60,000 starving prisoners. The camp held mainly Soviet prisoners of war and Jews.

Block Wardens In Nazi Germany, a person responsible for the local level political supervision of their neighbourhood. They would spread propaganda and spy on their neighbours.

Blomberg-Fritsch Affair Blomberg and Fritsch were the Minister of War and army Commander-in-Chief in the 1930s. Hitler felt they were insufficiently supportive of his desire for territorial expansion and war. In 1938, the two were forced to resign their positions after largely concocted sex scandals. Hitler used the opportunity of their resignations to increase his control over the army and establish a new Supreme Command of the armed forces in order to weaken the power of the traditional German army command structure.

Claims Conference Established in 1951 to seek compensation from the German government for the persecution and loss of property of Jews.

Cold War State of tension and conflict that existed between the USSR and its allies and the USA and its allies between approximately 1947 and 1990. The Cold War was characterised by hostility and competition over ideology, politics, arms and international influence. The two powers did not engage directly in war, hence the idea of a 'cold' war. They did, however, fight each other via proxies, for example in Vietnam and Afghanistan.

Concentration camp In Nazi Germany, camps where the Nazis held their opponents or others, such as racial minorities, who did not fit into their ideal for society.

Concordat Agreement signed between the Catholic Church and countries' governments.

Demilitarised Removing or not allowing a military force from an area, for example, the Rhineland after the First World War

denazification The Allied policy post-Second World War of attempting to rid German society and politics of the remnants of Nazism and Nazi ideas.

Einsatzgruppen SS Death squads who followed the German army as Germany conquered Eastern Europe and the Soviet Union carrying out mass killings of ideological and 'racial' enemies of the Nazis.

The Enlightenment Cultural movement to improve knowledge and reform and advance society.

Eugenics The idea, common in the first half of the twentieth century, that the genetic stock of humans can be improved through selective breeding. Eugenics often contained racist assumptions.

European Coal and Steel Community Organisation established in 1951 which was a forerunner of the EEC and which contained the same member states. It established a common market in coal and steel between members.

European Economic Community (EEC) Association of European countries, founded by the Treaty of Rome in 1957, aimed at promoting economic integration among members. The original members were West Germany, France, Italy, Belgium, the Netherlands and Luxembourg.

Federal Convention Constitutional assembly in West Germany which elected the President.

Freikorps Paramilitary (informal) groups of volunteer soldiers. In inter-war Germany these groups were often strongly nationalist and linked to extremist politics.

German Restitution Laws Laws passed in the 1950s which regulated the provision of the compensation of Jewish victims of the Nazis for persecution or loss of property.

Gleichschaltung Term referring to the process of co-ordination carried out by the Nazis after their accession to power. This co-ordination allowed the Nazis to extend their control over German institutions and parts of the state such as the civil service. The process could be regarded as one of nazification.

Grand Coalition Coalition government formed in 1928 in Germany. The government included representatives from left and right and was headed by Chancellor Muller of the SPD. The government was the longest lived of the Weimar Republic.

Hoover Moratorium Temporary end to the reparations payments that arose from the First World War, launched by US President Herbert H. Hoover in 1931. He was aiming to help relieve the world economic crisis.

Kristallnacht The Night of Broken Glass: an orchestrated wave of Nazi violence and attacks on Jewish people and property on 9–10 November 1938.

League of Nations International organisation of nation-states formed after the First World War with the aim of promoting disarmament and world peace.

Lebensraum Literally, 'living space'. Refers to the German aim of pursuing territorial expansion in Eastern Europe.

Luftwaffe German airforce.

Marshall Plan American aid programme for Western European which operated between 1948 and 1952, aimed at rebuilding countries, restoring trade and reducing the potential appeal to people of communism. In total, $13 billion was transferred from the USA to Europe.

Marxist Communist system of economic and political ideas founded by Karl Marx, which assumes that class struggle is a central part of history and social change and that political structures have economic bases; a belief in communal, collectivist politics.

Mixed economic model Economic system in which free enterprise co-exists alongside government intervention in the economy and government ownership of parts of the economy, for example, the railway and energy networks.

NATO North Atlantic Treaty Organisation – a pact between various countries, including Britain, France and the USA, to maintain each other security in the event of an attack by an aggressor. In the context of the Cold War, NATO entailed the United States guaranteeing Western Europe's security against a possible Soviet threat.

Nazi–Soviet Pact Non-aggression pact signed between Germany and the Soviet Union in August 1939 which meant that the Nazis could invade Poland without fear that the USSR would attack them. The pact also involved the definition of German and Soviet spheres of influence over parts of Eastern Europe and after the German invasion of Poland, the Soviets annexed parts of eastern Poland. The pact was ended by the German invasion of the Soviet Union in June 1941.

New Plan Nazi economic plan designed by Hjalmar Schacht and launched in September 1934. The plan aimed to reduce unemployment by providing government money to industry, reduce Germany's dependence on imports and stimulate trade by negotiating bilateral trade agreements with other countries.

Night of the Long Knives Name given to the occasion on 30 June 1934 when Hitler and members of the SS arrested and murdered Ernst Röhm and other SA leaders and the SA was brought under SS control. A number of other political opponents of the Nazis, like von Schleicher, were also murdered.

Non-aligned During the Cold War, countries allying themselves with neither the USSR's communist 'east', nor the USA's capitalist 'west'.

Nuclear proliferation Spread of countries possessing nuclear weapons.

Potsdam City adjacent to Berlin that was a seat of the Prussian Kings and German Kaiser until 1918.

Potsdam Conference Allied conference held in Potsdam after the end of the war in Europe, attended by Josef Stalin, leader of the USSR, Harry S. Truman, the new American president, and Winston Churchill, British Prime Minister, who was replaced by Clement Atlee of the Labour Party part way through the conference because the Labour Party had won the British general election. The Conference confirmed the division of Germany into zones of occupation, dealt with polices on denazification and determined the borders of Poland.

Proportional representation Electoral system in which seats allocated in parliament correspond exactly or very closely to the way in which people vote. For example, if 10 per cent of voters vote for a party, then that party receives 10 per cent of the seats in parliament.

Schutzstaffel **(SS)** Organisation that started off in the 1920s as Hitler's personal bodyguard, but expanded to become the main agent of terror in Nazi Germany. The SS were fiercely loyal to Hitler and his ideas. By 1934, the SS were rivals to the SA as the primary enforcers of Nazism. The SS were led by Heinrich Himmler and were responsible for repression and death camps in occupied territories in Eastern Europe during the Second World War.

Second Reich Name for the unified German state that existed between 1871 and 1918. It was a monarchical system, headed up by a Kaiser, with a democratic element. The Second Reich fell at the end of the First World War when, facing defeat and revolution, Kaiser Wilhelm II abdicated.

Sicherheitsdienst **(SD):** Intelligence agency of the SS.

SOPADE Term for the Social Democratic Party of Germany (SPD) in exile.

Treaty of Rome Agreement in 1957 that founded the EEC.

Volksgemeinschaft 'People's community' a Nazi concept entailing the unity of all members of the 'racial' community who adhered to Nazi ideology. The Nazis aimed to create a unified *Volksgemeinschaft* in Germany.

Warsaw Ghetto Jewish ghetto established by the Nazis in Warsaw, the Polish capital in 1940. The ghetto was closed to the outside world in November 1940. Conditions inside were extremely difficult and hundreds of thousands of people died of ill health and starvation. Others were later deported to death camps such as Treblinka. Following an uprising of remaining inhabitants in 1943, the ghetto was destroyed. Over 50,000 inhabitants of the ghettos were killed during or shortly after the uprising.

Wehrwirtschaft War economy.

Weltpolitik 'World politics': the German policy developed from the mid-1890s of seeking enhanced power and status in Europe and around the world through colonial and military expansion.

Key figures

Konrad Adenauer (1876–1967)   Christian Democrat leader and politician, Adenauer was Chancellor of West Germany from 1949 until 1963. He presided over Germany's transformation into a stable, peaceful and prosperous country after the Second World War.

Willy Brandt (1913–92)   Leading political figure in West Germany. He had been in exile during the Nazi era, and was head of the SPD and Chancellor from 1969–74. Brandt tried to strike a balance between a pro-American position for West Germany and improving relations with East Germany.

Frederich Ebert (1871–1925)   Saddle-maker, trade unionist, political activist and politician, Ebert was leader of the SPD party and the first President of Weimar Germany between 1919 and 1925. Ebert played a crucial role in the German revolution of 1918. As a moderate socialist, he acted to crush the communist Spartacists in 1919 and reach an accommodation with the German army.

Joseph Goebbels (1897–1945)   Leading Nazi politician and a close associate of Hitler. Goebbels was responsible for propaganda in Germany 1933 and 1945. He used modern technology to promote Nazi ideology and the idea that Hitler was a wise and all-knowing leader. In 1943, Goebbels persuaded Hitler to pursue a 'total war' strategy.

Heinrich Himmler (1900–45)   Leading Nazi politician and leader of the SS. Himmler became leader of the SS in 1929 and took this fanatical paramilitary organisation from its roots as Hitler's bodyguards and eventually made it the most powerful part of the Nazi state. The SS was the main organisation in charge of terror and ideological policy in Nazi Germany and was responsible for perpetrating the Holocaust. Along with Hitler, Himmler is one of the individuals most responsible for the Holocaust.

Paul von Hindenburg (1837–1934)   German general who was chief of the General Staff of the army during the First World War. Hindenburg was President of Germany between 1925 and his death in 1934. His politics were conservative and nationalist, and he was instrumental in both blocking Hitler's accession to the Chancellorship in 1932 and then in agreeing to bring Hitler and other Nazis into government in January 1933.

Adolf Hitler (1889–1945)   Austrian-born German fascist politician and leader of the NSDAP (Nazi Party) from 1921. He was Chancellor of Germany from 1933, and from 1934 became Führer, or dictator. He was instrumental in the development of anti-Semitic practices and policies in Germany and in the rise of tensions and conflict in Europe that culminated in the outbreak of Second World War. He was also instrumental in causing the Holocaust.

Helmut Kohl (1930–)   Chairman of the Christian Democrats and Chancellor of West Germany between 1982 and 1990 and reunited Germany between 1990 and 1998. Kohl is considered to be the main architect of the reunification of Germany and a leading figure in the establishment of the European Union.

Timeline

1918	November	Armistice ended the First World War and *Kaiser* Wilhelm II abdicated
1919	February	National Constituent Assembly formed and had its first meeting at Weimar; Friedrich Ebert elected President of the republic
	July	Spartacist uprising
1920	March	Kapp *Putsch*
1923	January	French and Belgian troops invade the Ruhr in response to Germany failing to meet reparation payments
	August	Gustav Stresemann becomes Chancellor and Foreign Minister
	November	Introduction of the Rentenmark, which helps end the inflation crisis
	November	Munich Beer Hall *Putsch*
1924	April	Dawes Plan agreed with the Allies
1925	April	General Hindenburg elected President
1929	February	Wall Street Crash
	June	Young Plan agreed with the Allies
1930	March	Heinrich Brüning becomes Chancellor; increasingly relies on Hindenburg's use of emergency powers to pass legislation
1932	April	Hindenburg beats Adolf Hitler convincingly during the presidential elections
	July	Nazis become the biggest party in the Reichstag
1933	January	Hitler is appointed Chancellor
	February	Reichstag fire
	March	Elections held and the Enabling Act passed
	July	All political parties disbanded apart from the Nazi Party
1934	June	Night of the Long Knives
	July	Schacht appointed Minister of Economics
	September	Schacht introduces the New Plan
	August	Death of Hindenburg and Hitler declared *Führer*
		Nazis centralise control over education policy
1936	October	Goering placed in charge of the Office of the Four-Year Plan
1938	March	*Anschluss* is announced with Austria
		Membership of the Hitler Youth becomes compulsory
	November	*Kristallnacht*
1939	September	Hitler invades Poland; Britain and France declare war on Germany
1941	June	Germany invades the USSR
1942	January	Wannsee Conference chaired by Heydrich decides Jews need to be eliminated through the establishment of death camps
1943	January	Germany defeated at Stalingrad
1945	May	Germany defeated in the Second World War and Hitler commits suicide
	June	Yalta Conference
	November	Beginning of Nuremberg Trials
1947		Truman Doctrine and Marshall Plan implemented
	January	Creation of Bizonia
1948	June	Berlin blockade and airlift begins
	June	Currency reform – introduction of Deutschmark
1949	May	Formation of the FRG
	August	Konrad Adenauer of the CDU/CSU becomes the first Chancellor of the FRG
	August	Appointment of Ludwig Erhard as Economics Minister
	October	GDR is established
		The Basic Law states that men and women are equal
1955		FRG joins NATO
1961		Berlin Wall begins to be constructed
1963	October	Adenauer resigns and is replaced by Ludwig Erhard
1966	December	Grand Coalition between the CDU/CSU and SPD headed by former Nazi Party member Kurt Kiesinger

1967	June	Stabilisation Law
1969	October	Willy Brandt of the SPD becomes Chancellor
1970		Escalation of violence against people by the Red Army Faction (RAF)
1972	September	Terrorist attacks at Munich Olympics
1974	May	Brandt resigns and is replaced by Helmut Schmidt
1982	October	CDU/CSU/FDP coalition established, headed by Chancellor Helmut Kohl
1989	November	Opening of the Berlin Wall
1990	October	GDR is abolished and formally reunited with the FRG
	December	First post-war all-German election returns Kohl as chancellor of a reunited Germany

Mark schemes

AO1 mark scheme

REVISED ☐

- **Analytical focus**
- **Accurate detail**
- **Supported judgement**
- Argument and structure

AS Marks		A-level Marks
1–4	Level 1 - Simplistic, limited focus - Limited detail, limited accuracy - No judgement or asserted judgement - Limited organisation, no argument	1–3
5–10	Level 2 - Descriptive, implicit focus - Limited detail, mostly accurate - Judgement with limited support - Basic organisation, limited argument	4–7
11–16	Level 3 - Some analysis, clear focus (may be descriptive in places) - Some detail, mostly accurate - Judgement with some support, based on implicit criteria - Some organisation, the argument is broadly clear	8–12
17–20	Level 4 - Clear analysis, clear focus (may be uneven) - Sufficient detail, mostly accurate - Judgement with some support, based on valid criteria - Generally well organised, logical argument (may lack precision)	13–16
	Level 5 - Sustained analysis, clear focus - Sufficient accurate detail, fully answers the question - Judgement with full support, based on valid criteria (considers relative significance) - Well organised, logical argument communicated with precision	17–20

AO3 mark scheme

REVISED ☐

- Interpretation and analysis of the extracts
- Knowledge of issues related to the debate
- Evaluation of the interpretations

AS Marks		A-level Marks
1–4	**Level 1** • Limited comprehension of the extracts demonstrated through selecting material • Some relevant knowledge, with limited links to the extracts • Judgement has little or no support	1–3
5–10	**Level 2** • Some understanding of the extracts demonstrated by describing some of their relevant points • Relevant knowledge added to expand on details in the extracts • Judgement relates to the general issue rather than the specific view in the question, with limited support	4–7
11–16	**Level 3** • Understanding of the extracts demonstrated through selecting and explaining some of their key points • Relevant knowledge of the debate links to or expands some of the views given in the extracts • Judgement relates to some key points made by the extracts, with some support	8–12
17–20	**Level 4** • Understanding of the extracts demonstrated through analysis of their interpretations, and a comparison of the extracts • Relevant knowledge of the debate integrated with issues raised by the extracts. Most of the relevant aspects of the debate are discussed – although some may lack depth • Judgement relates to the interpretations of the extracts and is supported by a discussion of the evidence and interpretations of the extracts	13–16
	Level 5 • Interpretation of the extracts demonstrated through a confident and discriminating analysis of their interpretations, clearly understanding the basis of both their arguments • Relevant knowledge of the debate integrated in a discussion of the evidence and arguments presented by the extracts. • Judgement relates to the interpretations of the extracts and is supported by a sustained evaluative argument regarding the evidence and interpretations of the extracts.	17–20

Answers

Page 7, Spot the mistake
At the end of the paragraph the answer should link back to the question.

Page 11, Eliminate irrelevance
It is not really accurate to say that the Weimar Republic's constitution undermined stability in Germany in 1919–29. Most of the problems that Weimar faced were nothing to do with the constitution. Although the constitution did add to political instability, as the PR system made it difficult to form durable governments, the main problems that Weimar faced were political extremism and economic problems that had nothing to do with the constitution. The political extremists included the Spartacists, ~~named after a Thracian gladiator~~, and the Nazi Party, led by Hitler. ~~Hitler was born in Braunau am Inn in Austria, and later lived in Vienna. His failed career as an artist had made him bitter.~~ The existence of the extremists was more a result of defeat in the war and not really to do with the Weimar constitution. Use of PR for the electoral system made it easier for extremists to gain representation in the Reichstag, but PR is a very democratic election system that did not cause the existence of extremists. So use of PR did not mean that the Weimar Republic's constitution was flawed from the outset.

Page 23, Support or Challenge?

	Support	Challenge
There were a number of attempts to overthrow the Weimar Republic including the Munich Putsch, the Kapp Putsch and the Spartacist Uprising		✓
The international community supported Weimar's survival via the Dawes Plan and the Young Plan		✓
The actions of Ebert and Stresemann helped the Republic to survive		✓
The opponents of Weimar lacked public support before 1930	✓	
There were a number of Communist uprisings in the Weimar Republic		✓
The attempts to overthrow the Republic were badly organised	✓	
Weimar's economy performed well between 1924 and 1929 and inflation was not a problem at this time	✓	

Page 25, Spot the mistake
At the end of the paragraph the answer should link back to the question.

Page 25 Support or challenge?

	Support	Challenge
Stresemann called off the passive resistance to French occupation in 1923, which helped restore some international confidence in Germany's economy	✓	
Stresemann negotiated the Dawes Plan, which saw money for investment flow into Germany	✓	
The international loans to Germany in the 1920s created a dangerous dependence on the United States		✓
Unemployment remained persistent throughout the 1920s		✓
The German economy did not grow as much as other economies between 1924 and 1929		✓
The German agricultural sector was in recession from 1927		✓

Quick quizzes at www.hoddereducation.co.uk/myrevisionnotes

Page 27, Eliminate irrelevance

The lives of some women were transformed in the Weimar era in Germany. Some young women living in urban areas, particularly Berlin, were able to live an independent and single life in a way that had not been possible before the First World War. This was all part of the more liberal and tolerant culture in Germany, and particularly in Berlin. ~~At this time there was a great deal of cultural experimentation in Germany, as can be seen in the art work of Kirchener, the designs of the Bauhaus and in the development of cabaret as an art form.~~ Furthermore, more women went to university and trained and worked in professions in this era. However, most women continued to occupy traditional roles within the family as wives and mothers, and many working-class women had worked before the Weimar era anyway, so the lives of these women were not transformed.

Page 29, Identify an argument

The second answer gets a higher mark.

Page 35, Identify a concept

How far do you agree that Weimar democracy was always likely to fail? SIGNIFICANCE

How accurate is it to say that the rise in unemployment was the most important consequence of the economic problems that Germany faced 1922–32? CONSEQUENCE

How accurate is it to say that the lack of support for democracy from Weimar's elite was responsible for Hitler's appointment to power? CAUSE

How far did the level of support for democracy in Germany change of the years 1919–32? CHANGE/CONTINUITY

Page 45, Support or challenge?

	Support	Challenge
Active resistance to the Nazi regime was rare in the 1930s	✓	
Non-conformity and dissent were relatively widespread		✓
There were some instances of protest against Nazi policies		✓
SOPADE reports suggest a high level of support for Hitler	✓	
There were some opposition groups, such as the Edelweiss Pirates and left-wing underground networks		✓
The Bomb Plot was an attempt to overthrow the Nazi regime in 1944		✓

Page 47, Spot the mistake

At the end of the paragraph, the answer should link back to the question.

Page 47, Support or challenge?

	SUPPORT	CHALLENGE
In 1935, 5,000 people in Germany were convicted of high treason		✓
100,000 people were held in concentration camps by the Nazis after they gained power		✓
Block Wardens monitored people on behalf of the Nazi party		✓
The Gestapo often relied on denunciations from the public	✓	
There is evidence that many Nazi policies were popular	✓	

Page 51, Support or challenge?

	SUPPORT	CHALLENGE
Some young women in Weimar Germany lived independent, self-supporting lives	✓	
The Nazis discouraged women from working and restricted women's places at university to 10 per cent	✓	
The Nazis encouraged and incentivised women to stay at home and have children	✓	✓
The number of women working increased during the 1930s		✓
Most women had a traditional role within the family during the Weimar era		✓
Women were banned from many professional occupations during the Nazi era	✓	

Page 83, Support or challenge?

	SUPPORT	CHALLENGE
War crimes trials brought some senior Nazis to justice	✓	
Denazification helped to reduce the appeal of Nazi ideas	✓	
Defeat in the war caused disillusionment with Nazi ideas	✓	
The Allies' denazification policy caused resentment in some Germans		✓
Denazification was a limited policy that left many people who had been active Nazis in positions of power and influence		✓

Page 85, Eliminate irrelevance

Constitutional Law was transformed in Germany between 1918 and 1949 to some extent. The Basic Law constitution introduced in 1949 was in part a return to the Weimar Constitution established in 1919, but it also contained important differences. ~~Weimar is a town in Germany where the constitution was written in 1919.~~ The Basic Law restored democracy to (West) Germany, and like the Weimar system, there were elections to the federal parliament every four years on the basic of universal suffrage. As in the Weimar system, the Chancellor and the government needed the support of the Parliament. However, there were various significant changes in the Basic Law in comparison with the Weimar Constitution which were designed to make democracy in the FRG stronger and more stable than that in Weimar Germany. One difference was that it was not so easy to remove a Chancellor through a vote of no confidence – a new government needed to be ready to be formed and in possession of sufficient support from Parliament. Furthermore, the new system reduced the proportional element in the voting system and made it harder for small extremist parties, such as the Nazis had been, to gain representation. ~~The Nazi Party was founded in 1919 in Munich by Anton Drexler.~~ The President, who was considered to have had too much power in the time of President Hindenburg, had very little power in the FRG, and could only appoint a Chancellor with Bundestag approval. Overall, the new constitution of the FRG was not a transformation in comparison with Weimar's constitution, but it did contain certain major modifications.

Page 97, Identify the key terms

The key terms are: 'strong popular support' in the first question and 'little effective opposition' in the second.

Page 99, Identify an argument

The first answer gets the higher mark.

Quick quizzes at www.hoddereducation.co.uk/myrevisionnotes

Notes